SHOPPER MARKETING

How to increase purchase decisions at the point of sale

Editors: Markus Ståhlberg and Ville Maila

KOGAN
PAGE

London and Philadelphia

First published in Great Britain and the United States in 2010 by Kogan Page Limited

120 Pentonville Road
London N1 9JN
United Kingdom
www.koganpage.com

525 South 4th Street, #241
Philadelphia PA 19147
USA

© Consultant editors and individual contributors, 2010

ISBN 978 0 7494 5702 0

British Library Cataloguing-in-Publication Data

A CIP record for this book is available from the British Library.

Library of Congress Cataloging-in-Publication Data

Stahlberg, Markus.
   Shopper marketing : how to increase purchase decisions at the point of sale / Markus Stahlberg, Ville Maila.
      p. cm.
   ISBN 978-0-7494-5702-0
   1. Advertising, Point-of-sale. 2. Marketing. 3. Consumers--Decision making. 4. Shopping--Decision making. I. Maila, Ville. II. Title.
   HF5828.S73 2010
   659.1′57--dc22
                                          2009022314

Typeset by Saxon Graphics Ltd, Derby
Printed and bound in India by Replika Press Pvt Ltd

Contents

Preface

The idea behind the shopper marketing book was born as a result of the constantly increasing number of enquiries from our clients around the globe about references to this hot new topic, shopper marketing. The fact that Phenomena Group, as a company, had extensive experience and insight on shopper marketing didn't seem to be enough for our clients – they wanted to know what was the best written source on the topic. I had no choice but to answer that, even though the different aspects of the discipline have been covered quite well in internet articles and books, not a single book dedicated solely to this new area of marketing was available. While doing research on the topic, I realized that shopper marketing had grown to be a significant global marketing phenomenon, something that could not have been foreseen in 2003 when our company, Phenomena Group, decided to focus on the area. From the very first moment when I got the idea of creating the book on shopper marketing I knew that I was about to commit to something very important, to a mission in completely uncharted territory.

The research on the book was commenced in August 2007 and I very quickly realized that the best results would be achieved if I humbly took advantage of the best experts in the different fields of shopper marketing globally, rather than trying to author the book based on my own experience. Instead of focusing on the numerous vague buzzwords and phrases so common in the field of marketing, I wanted to provide the readers with an in-depth insight directly from the actual practitioners of the discipline. I decided to approach a vast array of experts in different areas of shopper marketing in order to gain as extensive an outlook on the topic as possible. I am happy to say that I think the approach turned out to be quite successful!

The book was compiled during an exhaustive 20-month period. I engaged in relentless correspondence and face-to-face meetings with over 300 shopper marketing experts around the world. We ended up with 37 of the most prominent shopper marketing experts from four continents. Evaluating this intensive period afterwards, I realize that the information I have gathered exceeds that cumulated over my entire working history. I had to relinquish many myths regarding shopper behaviour and gained a more in-depth understanding of the nature of various new areas of shopper marketing. I am delighted to share the most important of these insights with you!

Markus Ståhlberg

Acknowledgements

I would like to express utmost gratitude to all authors who have contributed to this book. Special thanks go to Scott Young of Perception Research Services and Herb Sorensen of TNS Sorensen, who were happy to give their contributions at a very early stage of the process, when the concept of the book had only just been decided on. Additionally I would like to thank all the experts who didn't end up contributing to the book. They gave me a lot of additional insight and perspectives that helped immensely in formulating the book.

Thanks to my partners. First and foremost I would like to thank my long-time partner and friend Ville Maila, who introduced crucially important insights and expertise to the process. This book would not have been possible without him. Furthermore, I would like to give special thanks to Phenomena Group's experts, who supported and helped me during the 20-month process. They often helped me to get back on track with their comments regarding the principal objective of shopper marketing: increasing shoppers' purchase decisions.

Thanks to the publisher. Annie Knight from Kogan Page played an integral role in the creation of this book. Annie insisted on simplifying the messages in the book and getting rid of any irrelevant material. She kept her eye on the big picture, made sure we kept to our deadlines and made the more difficult things understandable.

Thanks to the loved ones. I would like to express my deepest gratitude to my beloved wife, Tia, and to our newborn baby, Mai. I couldn't have hoped for better support. This book would not have been possible without their understanding and support!

Dedicated to our amazing daughter Mai.

Markus Ståhlberg

Introduction

This is not a book about new marketing or advertising gimmicks. This book deals with something much more profound and important. This is a book about shopper marketing – about affecting shopper behaviour to generate purchase decisions.

Shopper marketing is growing faster than internet advertising – doubling in terms of investments since 2004 and on pace for a compound annual growth rate of 21 per cent to 2010, according to a draft study by Deloitte for the Grocery Manufacturers Association: 'Shopper marketing is a new medium as important as the internet, mobile or gaming.'

A good definition for shopper marketing, as a new marketing practice, can be found in Wikipedia: shopper marketing is 'understanding how one's target consumers behave as shoppers, in different channels and formats, and leveraging this intelligence to the benefit of all stakeholders, defined as brands, consumers, retailers and shoppers'.

Shopper marketing assumes that consumers and shoppers are not always – or even often – the same. For instance, a shopper for pet food products is highly unlikely to be the consumer.

In shopper marketing, manufacturers target portions of their marketing investment at specific retailers or retail environments. Such targeting is dependent on congruency of objectives, targets and strategies between the manufacturer and a given retailer or a given type of retail environment.

A significant factor in the rise of shopper marketing is the availability of high-quality data from which insights may be gleaned to help shape strategic plans. According to recent industry studies, manufacturer investment in shopper marketing is growing more than 21 per cent annually.

The following statistics have caused the reapportionment of marketing investment from consumer marketing to shopper marketing:

- Seventy per cent of brand selections are made at stores.
- Sixty-eight per cent of buying decisions are unplanned.

- Five per cent are loyal to the brand of one product group.
- Practitioners believe that effective shopper marketing is increasingly important to achieve success in the marketplace.

Shopper Marketing is the first book providing an extensive outlook into the various aspects of this new area of marketing. Because of the emerging nature of the new practice, the contents of the book are compiled from 37 global practitioners and professionals of shopper marketing. The extensive list of authors covers nearly all of the world-renowned experts of the area. The best way to approach the book depends on the nature of your interest in the topic, so there is no single correct way of reading it. For a comprehensive outlook on shopper marketing you may want to read the book from cover to cover, and for a quick insight on a specific topic you may want to dive into a few chapters at a time.

The contents of the book are divided into three parts:

1. Definition: what is shopper marketing?
2. Strategy: how to approach shopper marketing?
3. Execution: what is shopper marketing in action?

Marketers, by definition, have an inborn need to understand why their products are being purchased. This book serves as a beginning for understanding marketing from the shopper's purchase-decision point of view. Shopper marketing is related to the work of all marketing and sales professionals within the retail sector. For example, Microsoft, P&G, IBM, Unilever, the Coca-Cola Company and Nestlé have recently built internal units for shopper marketing. Shopper marketers aim to take advantage of the causal connections between shopping and purchase behaviour to create innovative concepts for increasing purchase decisions. As a part of our ongoing journey within the world of purchase decisions, we would highly appreciate readers' opinions. We would be delighted to respond to your questions, comments or challenges related to shopper marketing. We hope to hear from you for the possibility of learning something new together! You can find contact details for the Phenomena office nearest to you at www.phenomena.com.

Part 1
Definition: what is shopper marketing?

1 Science of shopping

Paco Underhill

Paco Underhill is founder, CEO and president of Envirosell. He has spent more than 25 years conducting research on the different aspects of shopping behaviour. Envirosell has established its reputation as an innovator in commercial research and as an advocate for consumer-friendly packaging and shopping environments.

I am a bald, nerdy, 54-year-old American research wonk. No one has ever thought of me as being fashionable. The woman I live with complains that my pants are routinely too short and my ties never match the suit I'm wearing – so banish me to Long Island! What I do know about is shops and shopping. My day job, which I've been doing for 23 years, is CEO of a testing agency for prototype stores. Envirosell, the company I founded and run, operates in 27 countries across the globe – in the past six months, my work has taken me from Dublin to Dubai.

If you'd asked me years ago whether I'd end up as a retail expert, I'd have asked you what insane asylum you'd escaped from. Then again, I've always been good at watching people. Growing up with a terrible stutter, I learned to look as a way of understanding social rules. I've turned a coping mechanism for a handicap into a profession (my mother just calls me an overpaid voyeur) for which I walk shops and malls across the world for a living. It is part Zen and part commerce.

As I stroll around, I look at store windows, since they are an essential part of the shopping experience. In his delightful book *Made in America*, Bill Bryson writes about the US national history of stores and shopping, describing the big picture windows that characterized turn-of-the-century retailing. When I look out of my office window in the

Ladies' Mile district of New York City, I see those same windows. They remain the same today as they were some 120 years ago, when cast-iron construction made the big window possible and reinvented the act of shopping.

A century ago, people took the time to stop and look into store windows. I imagine them strolling along, stopping at a tall window and peering through the glass, curious to view the latest fashions, just-arrived products or newest appliances. Today, the ambling window-shopping pedestrian may be an Edwardian concept. Most people look straight ahead and walk with a quick, determined gait. Everyone seems to be in a hurry. They walk a lot faster now than they did in the old days.

Throughout modern times, a number of factors have affected the average walking patterns of pedestrians in urban areas. One of the most significant of these is traffic signals. William H Whyte, the American author and urbanist, wrote at length about the platooning effect of pedestrian movement. He said that, with traffic lights set for the speed of cars, people pile up on street corners as they wait for the light to change. What often results from this pile-up is a pattern of light and dense patches of people moving down the sidewalks of urban shopping streets.

Now let's consider how individuals behave as they move within these dense patches of shopping humanity. Have you ever noticed that, whether you are on Chicago's Michigan Avenue or cruising your local mall, you and your fellow shoppers are able to move in incredibly dense clusters and not touch or bump into each other? Walking speeds, sidewalk density patterns, and the ways people behave when they walk in tight clusters have an important effect on the success of store windows, particularly in cities. Even if you did want to stop and look in a window, you would quickly be pushed past it, as you wouldn't want to risk disturbing the cluster you are walking with. That's why window displays need to instantly grab attention. But many don't. Take the CVS and Rite Aid drugstores that blanket my neighbourhood. I wonder in which century the merchandise managers were born. The windows are so crowded with boxes of bleach and detergent, packages of razors and soap on sale, six-packs of soda, cosmetics, hair goo, and whatever else can be squeezed into the window space that it is impossible to focus on any single product or even see clearly what is really being promoted!

Maybe in 1928 it was important for a drugstore to advertise depth of selection or the range of products offered. Maybe then shoppers had the time and solitary moments of shopping to really take a look at a window and examine the display. Maybe then crowded windows made more sense. But, these days, merchandisers are lucky if pedestrians give their store windows a passing glance. Windows must be quick reads if you expect busy shoppers walking in dense clusters to see them. They must be both simple enough so that the products can be clearly identified and creative enough to catch the busy pedestrian's eye. Savvy shoppers should be able to tell, just by briefly looking at a store window, who the core market of that store is, whether the store fits their personal style or not, and how long a typical trip inside the store will take. Especially as today's retail market is so highly competitive, if done properly windows can function as an important brand-identity tool. A clever, catchy, clear window can be the result of the best and most effective marketing dollars you spend.

Unfortunately, many major store chains still have no idea what a good window means and how it can contribute to their store's success. Instead, from New York City to the local strip mall, from drug market to mass market, from video rental to jewellery shop, the store window is fast becoming a lost art form and a neglected marketing tool. While fashion retailers pay more attention to windows than other industries, they, too, have their own failings. At many apparel chains, window designers create standard, monthly windows for all stores, regardless of the size or location of an individual store. Even when designers create fancy flagship stores that resemble retail palaces, they often completely ignore the state of their street frontage – by far the most highly visible part of the store.

What makes a good window isn't getting easier to describe. But it does start with an understanding that, while the average overall vision of 'first world' citizens is deteriorating thanks to an ageing population, the general connection between our eyes and our brains is getting much more sophisticated. Thanks to television, film and computers, our ability to process images and icons is improving. We no longer read letter by letter but, rather, word clump by word clump. In the 1930s, French essayist André Bazin wrote about how cinematic language evolved so that movies successfully and believably told the stories of years – or even lifetimes – in the span of just a few hours. Today, MTV has pushed that evolution, taking visual poetry into a mainstream vocabulary that viewers truly understand. A billboard can tell a more sophisticated joke today than it could 20 years ago. A 15-second commercial can allude to an entire plotline. Likewise, when it comes to window displays, shoppers today can infer and understand more from less because they possess an enormous vocabulary of visual images. Yet the mainstream window-design profession still doesn't get it.

As retailers, you must be tactical; you must know who your customer is, and you must create a window that he or she will understand. For instance, Kiehl's, which sells all-natural bath and body products, uses its windows as a pulpit for highlighting social issues, a practice perfectly aligned with the priorities of its customers.

My favourite windows are in France. I know a man who runs his family's boutique off the main square in Strasbourg. He takes enormous pleasure in his windows. They tell jokes. They have political messages. They relate history. The clothes are part of the plot. Sometimes his windows make me chuckle. His store always distinguishes itself among all of the shops on the crowded square because his windows always make an impression. As busy as I might be as I walk down the street, his windows make me stop in my tracks. Even more, they almost always tempt me to come inside the shop and take a good look around.

So to modern retailers I propose the following: let's liberate our design teams. Let's take our lessons from Absolut Vodka's legendary advertisements, Calvin Klein's dark, clever ads and Benetton's stridently correct ones. Windows can be like literature. It's OK if not everybody gets the story you're telling. What is important is that the target customer gets it.

2 Point of view on shopper marketing

Gordon Pincott

Gordon Pincott is chairman of Global Solutions at Millward Brown. For over 25 years he has been actively involved in the strategic planning and research evaluation of brands and communications. Millward Brown is one of the world's leading research companies, with offices in more than 50 countries, and expert in marketing research and brand consulting.

Introduction

Shopper marketing is becoming an increasing focus for many of the world's major brands. Reaching people using traditional means has become more difficult. Media audiences have fragmented and people are increasingly annoyed by unsolicited advertising intrusions. But all consumers will eventually arrive at the point of purchase.

A 2007 study conducted by Deloitte in the United States suggests that the portion of marketing budgets devoted to point-of-purchase activity doubled from 3 per cent in 2004 to 6 per cent in 2007, and is expected to reach 8 per cent by 2010.

Defining shopper marketing

More often than not 'shopper marketing' is directed toward exactly the same person whom brands target outside of stores with TV and other forms of activity. But too often we observe a complete lack of integration between in-store and out-of-store activity. After all, when consumers enter a store as 'shoppers', they do not suddenly become blank slates. They arrive in a particular mood, having chosen this particular retail outlet to fulfil their particular mission. They arrive with opinions concerning quality and value. But, even more importantly, they arrive with well-developed preferences for brands, based on associations built up over time from advertising messages, word of mouth and personal experience. On average around two-thirds of people know what brand they want to buy before they go into the store. About three-quarters of these 'intenders' follow through on their plans. For shopper marketing to be effective, then, it needs to work with the predispositions people bring with them to the store. Two broad strategies that can be employed to effect this are identification and disruption.

Strategy one: identification

For brands that are the preferred choice of many consumers, the key point-of-purchase task is to make them as easy as possible for shoppers to find. In a bricks-and-mortar store, the location, scale and visibility of the fixture, as well as the location and prominence of the brand within the fixture, are essential factors.

In online retailing, the dynamics of identification are no different, but it is also critical to think about how the brand will be presented online. Will shoppers readily identify a brand from a tiny packshot, a logo or a description?

Regardless of whether shoppers are in-store or online, many factors could undermine the identification strategy, such as a change of product location or packaging. An increase in price will cause the shopper to hesitate and consider alternatives, and of course the ultimate sin is to be out of stock.

Strategy two: disruption

Disruption often takes the form of out-and-out bribery through a variety of financial incentives such as 'buy one get one free' and price reduction, but may also be accomplished through other in-store activities that attract attention and highlight a brand's unique benefits. When black and silver were the predominant colours in the consumer electronics category, Apple's choice of the colour white for the original iPod helped set that product apart from competing brands.

The role of packaging

Often, the development and evaluation of packaging are focused on its ability to communicate messages about the brand. But that is not where the power of packaging lies. The familiar visual cues of well-known brands are powerful not because they communicate specific messages, but because they are distinctive and instantly recognizable.

By understanding a brand's core iconography, packaging and point-of-sale materials, it is then possible to extend and connect a brand's out-of-store communication to the store shelf.

What role do in-store media have to play?

The aforementioned Deloitte report suggests that 'stores should be thought of like any other marketing media', but the busy environment of a retail outlet is no place for the equity-building work that can be accomplished outside of the store. While shopping, people are in a different mindset from that of watching TV or reading a magazine. In situations where shoppers want to be informed, engaged or entertained, some new forms of in-store media may work well, but often shoppers do not want to be distracted.

In a task-driven shopping environment, communication must be tightly focused, with short, clear, relevant messaging, seeking either to rekindle existing brand associations or to present a simple, compelling reason to choose a brand.

Strategy three: enticement

There is a third key in-store strategy, 'enticement'. Via store layout, presentation, design and lighting, shoppers are encouraged to spend more time browsing categories they may not have been thinking about when they entered the store.

Unable to compete with Wal-Mart on price, a number of major US supermarket groups are reinventing themselves as more relaxed and comfortable places to shop. Taken to an extreme, enticement can become a form of 'retail-tainment'. The queues that form outside the Apple store on Fifth Avenue provide a vision of what is possible if you sell a desirable product range in a compelling retail environment.

However, the notion of enticing the shopper is not compatible with the idea that the retail environment is a place where manufacturers can bombard consumers with aggressive marketing messages. Communications are most effective when they fit the needs and moods of consumers.

The shopper: same person, different context

We need to integrate our thinking and our actions so that what we do in the store dovetails with what we do outside. There are two keys to unlocking the power of shopper marketing. The first is to develop communications within the point of purchase that acknowledge that the mindset and motivation of a person shopping are very different from the mindset of someone watching, reading or listening to ads at home. The second is to build presence in the store, with a robust understanding of the brand associations that already exist in the minds of consumers as the result of communication outside of the store.

Shopper marketing should be a seamless part of the marketing discipline, considered and developed in conjunction with all the other marketing elements. There is a huge opportunity for those who reach out to achieve this.

3 Shopper marketing: the discipline, the approach

Jim Lucas

Jim Lucas currently serves as director of the shopper marketing group at Draftfcb, providing expertise on consumers and retail environments for product marketers and retailers. Draftfcb is one of the largest global advertising agency networks, with its headquarters in both New York and Chicago.

Over the next few years, retail will change quickly and dramatically. To survive, the store has to become its own brand. Strong brands provide a unique shopping experience and differentiate a store from its competition, and create shopper loyalty. For manufacturers to survive in an environment where retailers are devoting more time and space to talking about their store brand, the manufacturer must align with retailers in creating a unique shopping experience.

In view of this situation, shopper marketing can be thought of as a discipline (generating insights and understanding shoppers) and as an approach (an intuitive understanding of shoppers that allows us to act). Deploying the two sides of shopper marketing we hope to make it clearer just what shopper marketing is and the role insights play.

The overall process can be thought of as follows:

- 3Ss – defining the issue and objective:
  - shelf;
  - shopper;
  - store;
- go-to-market calendarization.

3Ss approach

Shelf

The shelf serves as our starting point. The issues or challenges we identify at the shelf help establish the 'behavioural objectives' and therefore set the strategic direction. We are using 'shelf' figuratively here. Shelf may refer to a category, a department or an aisle.

There are a number of major behavioural objectives we may be trying to achieve. The nature of the specific shelf will help determine where the greatest challenge or opportunity is. For example, in the 'centre of store' one of the biggest challenges is to drive aisle turn-in. Below are six common behavioural objectives:

1. store traffic – how to get the shopper to visit the store;
2. sales receipt – the total amount of purchase;
3. aisle turn-in – how we get shoppers to visit an aisle, category or department;
4. category sales – sales from a single category, shelf or department;
5. shelf 'stickiness' – how we get better engagement at the shelf or better navigation, education or inspiration;
6. sales conversion – how we can improve sales conversion.

A typology of purchase decisions (from highly involved to habitual) suggests that the buying process is affected by the type of item purchased. High-involvement purchases involve more pre-search, more sources, the exploration of more options and more time than low-involvement purchases. More complicated or involved categories (eg consumer electronics, skin care, and dieting or weight management) often require more in the way of shopper education or an inspiration or enablement approach. On the other hand, less involved or more 'habitually purchased categories' may simply benefit from an easier shopping experience or better navigation.

Based on in-store observational research of four different categories (categories masked for confidentiality), Table 3.1 shows how shelves vary in the issues they face and the kind of behaviour that must be carried out. Category A has many forms, brands and fragrances and therefore challenges shoppers browsing the shelf. They spend a relatively long time at the shelf and make comparisons, and so on. This suggests that better education or organization of the shelf could help improve shopping. In contrast, category B has a low browse time and relatively little comparison. This seems to be much more of a 'grab and

Table 3.1 Shelf profiles

Category	Comparison of different shelf profiles				
	Time spent at shelf (seconds)	Single product	Grab and go	Compared two or more brands	Conversion rate
Category A	50	72	23	55	33
Category B	25	92	47	28	40
Category C	30	87	32	30	30
Category D	35	65	27	40	25

go' category with a high conversion rate, suggesting not a high level of involvement or consideration.

Another way to think about the shelf is in terms of what Schwartz (2004) has referred to as the paradox of choice – the fact that more choice is often less helpful or desirable. More choice is desirable up to a point, but once it exceeds the threshold it becomes cumbersome and actually curtails purchase. The challenge is: how can retailers and manufacturers improve the shopping experience, eg relevant assortment editing, more intuitive shelf organization, better education, enablement or inspiration at the shelf?

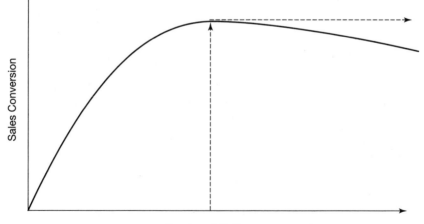

Figure 3.1 Law of diminishing returns

Shopper

A focus on the shopper not only provides the best source of insight, but serves as an important tool for aligning the retailer and manufacturer. The shopper helps unite retailer and manufacturer in terms of both their shopper understanding and their ability to deliver relevant communications in-store.

A useful way to study the shopper is to map the path to purchase. The mapping of the purchase path often utilizes a wide variety of research. This mapping typically goes beyond the store to help identify critical junctures in the purchase process where relevant information and experience can be best delivered to shoppers (eg home, store, etc).

The first path-to-purchase example is for flat screen TVs. Building the purchase path using a diverse range of shopper information (eg observational research, surveys and secondary research), one begins to see how the decision process unfolds. The flat screen TV purchase is relatively involved and expensive. The purchase path is not very linear. Shoppers turn to a number of sources and visit a number of retailers before making their purchase. The shopper and store associate are looking for useful information to aid their decision. Increasingly, this has evolved away from features toward benefits (eg less intrusive in-room decor, different aspect ratio to traditional TV, high-quality picture, better experience, etc).

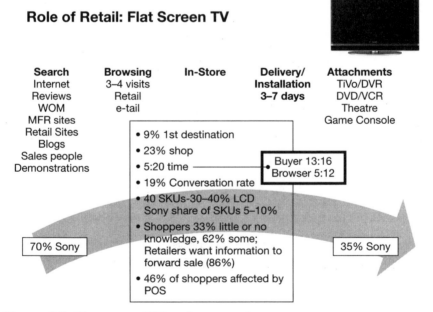

Figure 3.2 Flat screen TV path to purchase

While this information has been modified for confidentiality, note that the proportion of shoppers who claim to want to purchase a specific flat screen TV brand going into the store is about twice as large as the percentage who actually purchase.

In the case of more traditional CPG products (eg trips that involve the supermarket, mass merchandiser, hypermart or price club), the path to purchase may be more complex because one is trying to affect a single purchase, within the larger trip involving multiple purchases. Shoppers are likely to take on a host of roles during the shopping trip (eg purchasing agent, nutrition officer, hero, global citizen, etc).

The availability of new research methods for studying shopper in-store behaviour (eg observational research, tracking via shopping cart or RFID, use of sensors or video cameras) has greatly aided our ability to develop purchase paths.

The typical supermarket trip illustrates a somewhat different situation for many CPG brands. The typical or average supermarket trip takes about 30 minutes. The window of opportunity determines how and what we communicate to the shopper in the store (this varies across different types of retail). During that time shoppers are shopping for an average of six or seven different categories and walk out with 10 or 11 items. About 10 per cent of this time is devoted to the checkout. Often, if working with a CPG manufacturer, we are trying to affect a small portion of the shopping trip.

CPG Path to Purchase:
Average Supermarket Shopping Trip

Figure 3.3 CPG supermarket path to purchase

Understanding of the purchase path helps the development of the message hierarchy (prioritization of messaging). The message hierarchy reflects the decision tree, though the order may be somewhat different. At its simplest, the message hierarchy tries to attract or pique, engage or educate, and induce action.

Path to purchase also identifies areas and sequences in the purchase path where shoppers need help or are open to suggestions. The purchase path provides a means for retailers and manufacturers to map out their messaging strategies in the store. The resulting message map specifies what should be communicated in different areas and sequences in the shopping trip.

Store

The store is a medium. Like other media, it has a format, an audience (shoppers) and editorial content (retail brand and/or shopping experience). Typically, when undertaking a shopper marketing project, one must develop somewhat different approaches for different retailers, not unlike a magazine ad, which is tailored to different magazines and audiences. It is important to understand how, when and where to affect the retailer's shoppers (eg circulars, loyalty cards, cross-merchandising and cross-promoting, the shelf, secondary and tertiary displays).

Today's store is a brand. Thus, each retailer has a different focus. Kroger and Tesco have a greater focus on delivering shopper value via their dunnhumby loyalty programme, while other retailers may have a greater focus on other areas (eg Whole Foods Market on natural and organic, Safeway on lifestyles, Costco on treasure hunt, HEB's Central Market on food theatre or Publix Sabor on Hispanic lifestyle). So it is critical to know what retailers are trying to achieve with their brands or shopping experience.

What role does the category or shelf play for the retailers (eg destination category, impulse area, inspiration, etc)? Moreover, how does this category fit with the retailer's calendar as well as the things the shopper is doing with the category during different times of the year?

Go-to-market calendarization

The calendar plays a critical role in the go-to-market process. The calendar incorporates shopper insights, retailer focus and brand news throughout the year. Typically, individual calendars are developed for each key retail account.

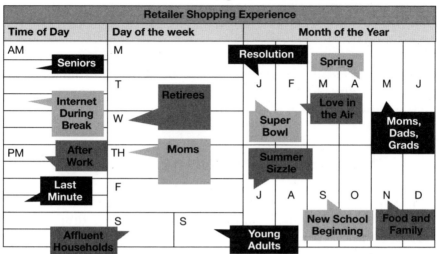

Figure 3.4 Calendarization

By using a calendar approach, we ensure that each event in a calendar supports the overall shopping experience or store as a brand. Align the needs of the shopper, retailer and manufacturer on the calendar and leverage the equities or assets each has. The calendar also helps identify the best vehicles for a shopper segment, retailer or time period.

Conclusion

The two faces of shopper marketing (discipline and approach) were brought together. Shopper marketing at its essence is about improving the shopping experience. It is also about making the experience unique to a retailer. The 3Ss approach is a process designed to help achieve improvements:

- When addressing a specific problem of category, it is important to recognize that each shelf or category is unique. Starting with the shelf or category, we can define behavioural objectives that help both manufacturer and retailer attain their business goals.
- Better understanding of shopper thought and behaviour is essential to the process. The shopper is a consumer in a unique mode, so the challenges are sometimes different from those of consumers. It is important to employ a range of research (behavioural, attitudinal, etc) to understand the shopper and identify opportunities.

● Understanding the store as a medium and a brand helps one to deliver solutions that are relevant to the shopper, retailers and manufacturer. The store also serves as the key for delivering the solution.

Finally, the calendar is a go-to-market tool that aids coordination and strategic alignment and identifies the most appropriate vehicles for specific shopper segments, retailers and time periods.

Reference and further reading

Hui, S, Bradlow, E and Fader, P (2007) An integrated model of grocery store shopping path and purchase behavior (unpublished manuscript)

Inman, J, Ferraro, R and Winer, R (2004) Where the rubber meets the road: a model of in-store consumer decision making (unpublished manuscript)

IRI (2006) *Time and Trends*, IRI, Chicago, IL

Moseman, T (2006) *Changing Channels*, Envirosell, New York

Schwartz, B (2004) *The Paradox of Choice: Why more is less*, HarperCollins, New York

4 Seven steps towards effective shopper marketing

Luc Desmedt

Luc Desmedt is managing director at LD & Co, where he specializes in delivering consulting projects that consist of the development of sales and trade marketing competence and strategies. LD & Co offers training and consulting services, aimed at helping manufacturers in developing and implementing the commercial skills they need to deal successfully with retailers.

Shopper marketing has become a strategic priority for most manufacturers. But for many consumer goods companies, the road to a successful implementation of this activity proves difficult. In order to help brand manufacturers implement effective shopper marketing, LD & Co has developed a pragmatic approach building on seven steps.

Since the early 1990s, POPAI research in several countries and product categories has shown time and again that the vast majority of actual purchase decisions are taken in-store – and this is despite major above-the-line advertising efforts by manufacturers to influence brand preference and purchase behaviour.

For a long time, only a few front-runners like P&G, Unilever and Kraft Foods considered the point of sales to play a strategic role in their commercial strategies. But, as the media landscape gets more and more fragmented, it has become very difficult for manufacturers to communicate successfully with demanding consumers via the traditional advertising channels. As a result, winning at the 'first moment of truth', as P&G calls it, is today a key priority for basically all manufacturers in food, but also more and more in non-food as well. However, understanding the importance of the point of sales is one thing; successfully addressing this priority is yet another challenge.

First of all, the shop floor is owned by professional retailers, for whom marketing has evolved from a tactical activity to a positioning and strategy-defining discipline. Needless to say, they also understand the power of their shop floor to reach the shopper effectively. In other words, when aiming at exploiting the point of sales as a marketing platform, manufacturers have to understand the retailer's marketing priorities and then try to match these with their own objectives when developing shopper marketing strategies and activities.

Another important prerequisite for successful shopper marketing is the availability of the right competence and dedicated resources. This might seem to be quite obvious, but in reality it turns out often to be a key bottleneck. Given its specific nature, shopper marketing requires a solid mix of strategic marketing skills and pragmatic, tactical sales skills. Shopper marketers must be able to understand the vision and objectives of their marketing department, generate the relevant shopper and retailer insights and mix all these elements into a smart and perfectly executed point-of-sales proposition.

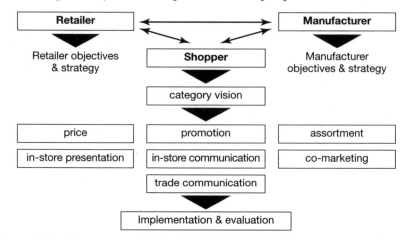

Figure 4.1 Shopper marketing framework

Developing shopper marketing plans and activities is not something that brand marketers or key account managers should do on top of their regular tasks. The strategic importance and the complexity of the work call for dedicated employees who work closely with marketing and sales.

Additionally, moving into shopper marketing assumes a proactive, structured and well-founded planning process:

- *Proactive:* shopper marketing activities should be the outcome of an accurate analysis that has indicated at which retailer it is appropriate to do which activity as a result of a well-defined strategy. Too often a shopper marketing activity is the opportunistic response to a request of a retailer on the occasion of a special event.

- *Structured:* the development of a shopper marketing strategy should be part of the manufacturer's business planning process, consisting of a flow of analytical, alignment, development and implementation steps.
- *Well-founded:* as for any marketing initiative, the potential of shopper marketing will be optimal if the development of the strategy and plans is facts based, ie building on an in-depth understanding of the business dynamics and the availability of relevant consumer, shopper and retailer insights.

In order to help manufacturers in establishing a pragmatic shopper marketing development process in their commercial organization, LD & Co developed an approach, which builds on seven steps.

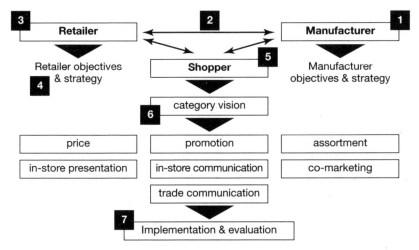

Figure 4.2 LD & Co seven-step approach

Step one: start with the corporate and marketing objectives and strategies

Whatever is communicated to the shopper at the point of sales obviously needs to be fully consistent with the brand strategy and in line with the brand communication via other media channels. In practice, however, there are often so many steps between strategy and in-store execution or so many different people involved in the process that crucial strategic details get lost or forgotten along the way. Therefore a clear understanding of the manufacturer's brand essentials should be a must for everyone who is involved in the development and implementation of shopper marketing activities.

Step two: make the right choices

Resources are limited, and it's impossible to do everything with every retailer. It should not be the most demanding retailer or key account manager who has most influence, who should attract the most attention and resources. The decision as to which level of focus and attention will be attributed to which retailer should be based on a careful screening of each retailer, taking into account three key criteria (Cijs and van den Berg, 2007):

1. The economic value of the retailer to the manufacturer.
2. Target consumer value: to what degree can the manufacturer reach its target consumer via the retailer?
3. Collaborative opportunities: to what degree is the retailer prepared to work in an open and constructive way?

To answer these questions properly, a manufacturer needs to have the data and systems to deliver the right information, which often turns out to be a barrier.

Step three: get an in-depth understanding of the current business situation at the key retailers

'One size fits all' clearly does not work for shopper marketing. Shopper marketing can only be effective if the activity succeeds in combining the brand's interests with the category opportunities for the retailer. In order to detect these opportunities, an in-depth business analysis of the category at the retailer is a must. Key questions that need to be addressed are: what is the business situation of the manufacturer at the retailer, and what is the performance of the retailer within the category? For both questions the key challenge is then to find the 'why' behind the diagnosed situation by analysing assortment, pricing, in-store presentation, and promotions. To answer these questions and draw the right conclusions, manufacturers need the right analytical skills and the discipline to make analysis part of the regular business planning process. Experience shows that these requirements still represent a key bottleneck for quite a few manufacturers.

Step four: get an in-depth understanding of key retailers' organization, objectives and strategies

Another key factor for successful shopper marketing activities consists of the commitment of the retailer. Retailers will be motivated to give full support to an initiative when they see clear benefits for themselves: activities that help them in achieving their marketing objectives and that respect their operational standards and ways of working. For manufacturers, this implies not only an in-depth understanding of the retailers' objectives and strategies, but also productive relationships across different departments, functions and levels. True retailer understanding is often an underestimated asset, which can be developed only via a planned and structured approach in which different people, from different functions and levels, have a role to play.

Step five: know the shoppers and their shopping behaviour

Basically every manufacturer of consumer goods today understands that consumer insights represent the basics for successful product development and marketing support. Logically the same goes for shopper marketing. In addition, having an in-depth understanding of shopping behaviour at key retailers often represents an important key to opening interesting doors within the organization of retailers.

Although there are clearly some commonalities between consumer and shopper understanding, they are nevertheless two different games, which each require a specific approach in terms of methodology, information resources to consult, business questions to be answered, and analysis. Shopper understanding basically needs to enable the shopper marketer to find out which type of shopper buys the category at which channel or retailer during which type of shopping trip, and how and why. This information then needs to be interpreted in the right way to detect key insights. It's clear that this again requires the appropriate analytical skills and the necessary funds to collect the required information.

For some manufacturers, allocating money for shopper research is still a tough battle, and other manufacturers sometimes get carried away by shopper research. Shopper research should be a means to effective shopper marketing and not an objective as such. Therefore precisely defining the information needs, which are based on the key opportunities and detected via the analysis of the business at the selected retailers, should be a key responsibility of every shopper marketer. And taking into account that leading retailers get to know their shoppers better and better thanks to the structured analysis of loyalty card databases, this responsibility becomes even more important.

Step six: develop a shopper marketing strategy and plan as part of tailored and complete account plans

The previous five steps are preparatory steps, aimed at collecting the information that is required to develop the basis upon which to build, via this step, a well-founded commercial strategy. The resulting strategy should clearly specify what to do at which retailer, starting from the manufacturer's corporate and marketing objectives and taking into account the identified retailer and shopper needs. In this way, shopper marketing activities are part of a larger, synergetic framework. It should be the ambition of every shopper marketer to develop and implement activities that use the impact of all the manufacturer's efforts at and around the point of sales. Developing creative solutions to address the identified opportunities is the key ingredient to achieve this. Unfortunately, creativity often seems to be ignored or is absent when thinking about shopper marketing.

Step seven: execute with excellence and measure the results

As is widely known, the proof of the pudding is in the eating! A shopper marketing activity can reflect a brilliant concept, but success will ultimately depend on how the activity hits the shopper. Hence the job is not done when the activity is sold to a buyer or a category manager at a retailer's headquarters. The most crucial part of the process, ensuring a perfect execution, is then to be started. In reality this means paying attention to a variety of small details to make sure that the right products get to the point of sales at the right time and in the right place. This assumes, for instance, a good knowledge of the retailer's logistics process, a field sales force that is briefed to implement or to check the in-store execution, and proactive and clear communication to all the people involved.

And last, but not least, everything can be improved. Therefore measuring and understanding the impact of shopper marketing represent a key, but often neglected, pillar for future success.

Reference

Cijs, R and van den Berg, H (2007) *The Trade Marketing Dimension*, Academic Service, The Hague

5 Bringing shopper into category management

Brian Harris

Dr Brian Harris is recognized around the world as the 'father of category management'. He is founder and chairman of the Partnering Group. The Partnering Group is a company that develops and implements his category management business methods.

There is no doubt, in my opinion, that shopper marketing represents the 'next wave' in the evolution of retail marketing concepts and methods. Its time has come and the reasons for its emergence at this time seem clear. The primary purpose of this chapter is to support the proposition that 'shopper marketing is the next wave' by briefly tracing the history of retail marketing 'waves' that have preceded shopper marketing. Of particular importance is the foundation that has been provided for shopper marketing over the last 20 years by the successful implementation of the consumer-focused philosophy and business processes of category management. Understanding the logical evolution from category management to shopper marketing, I believe, will accelerate the development and acceptance of this next exciting era of retail marketing.

Looking back over the history of modern retail marketing, there is one clear conclusion. In the world of retail marketing, changes occur in an evolutionary, not a revolutionary, manner. The intensity of competition, the narrow profit margins, the impact of relatively high fixed costs on break-even points, and the difficulty of changing traditional consumer shopping patterns have given most retail companies hesitation when contemplating any change that might be more revolutionary in nature. The pattern of change therefore has been more one of evolution. Shopper marketing represents the latest wave in this evolution of modern retail marketing that started in the 1970s. I like to use the term 'waves' to describe these changes for several reasons. First, waves have patterns and interconnections. The current wave helps shape the next wave. By better understanding the current wave, retailers and manufacturers can better position themselves to take advantage of the next wave. Second, being first to recognize the next wave usually brings competitive advantages.

As Figure 5.1 shows, since the mid-1970s there has been a series of important industry-changing waves in the area of retail marketing. The first wave was set in motion in the mid-1970s by the introduction of POS scanning technology and the new data these systems began to provide retailers and manufacturers. This information provided new insights into the results of key tactical decisions retailers and manufacturers make to increase the sales and profits of their stores and products. For the first time, opportunities for improving shelf space management, assortment, promotion, and pricing decisions could be identified and supported by data rather than based on traditional, often more emotion-based, decision-making methods.

These new data, especially when combined with the introduction of the personal computer in the early 1980s, paved the way for the next wave – the availability of the first PC-based tools that analysed POS data to measure the results of retail decisions. The development and widespread adoption of shelf space management systems, Apollo and Spaceman being the first of these systems, characterized this wave.

Retail Marketing – The Big Waves

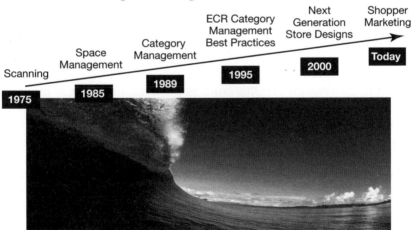

Figure 5.1 Retail marketing – the big waves

Category management, which I first introduced in 1989 (Harris, 1989), represented the next wave. The growing use and success of these PC-based tactical tools demonstrated the opportunity to broaden the application of these kinds of tools to the full spectrum of retail tactical decisions (assortment, promotion and pricing, as well as shelf space management). What was needed was a more strategic framework and a business process within which these tools were used as part of a total management system. These tools also supported the emerging objective of some leading retailers of developing more strategic consumer-based marketing capabilities within their organizations. Category management, with its focus on the consumer and 'the category as a strategic business unit', provided the philosophy and business process to achieve this objective.

The widespread adoption and successful use of category management provided the foundation for the next wave of retail marketing – the design of new, more shopper-friendly retail store formats. Category management evolved from its initial focus on the individual category to a multi-category, or portfolio, with its focus centred on consumer 'solution centres'. New store designs were developed based on store layouts configured around a set of solution centres anchored by 'destination' role categories. The principles of category management had evolved from a category to a total store application. Retailers such as Wegmans, Tesco, Wal-Mart and Best Buy were early adopters of these new retail store design concepts. The consumer-focused and strategy-oriented processes of category management provided the foundation for these new store designs. The success of one wave created the foundation for the next wave. This logical evolution now continues with the next wave – shopper marketing – which is about understanding and meeting the needs of the shopper at the point of purchase (or at the 'moment of truth' as Procter & Gamble has rightly described it).

What factors are driving the emergence of shopper marketing? Some of these reasons are the same as those that led to the introduction of category management almost 20 years ago. At the heart of any new management method is the constant search, by retailers and manufacturers, for sources of competitive advantage. Shopper marketing, like category management, represents an opportunity to use the competitive strengths of companies that believe in early-mover strategies for competitive advantage. These competitive strengths arise from forward-thinking management in combination with the impact of a number of other influences, including information and technology advantages, emerging competitive threats, and superior collaborative capabilities. In the case of category management, the initial adopters typically also had a history of innovative leadership in the adoption of other new approaches and methods. Many also had advantages in the availability and use of new information sources (in this case, with POS or scanning data) and an enlightened awareness of the advantages of better collaboration with trading partners. This combination of factors provided key components of the platform needed for success against the inroads of the then new and emerging competition, the discount mass merchandisers (such as Wal-Mart) and 'category killers'. What was needed was a business concept and process to put these elements into practice. Category management, with its core concept of 'the category as a strategic business unit' and its category planning business process, provided this platform.

In the case of shopper marketing, we see a number of similar factors at work. The continual search for competitive advantage will again lie at the centre of interest for this new concept. Again it will be a relatively small number of retailers and manufacturers that will lead the adoption and disproportionately influence the shape of this emerging management approach. In a way that is akin to the role that POS data played in paving the way for category management, shopper marketing will capitalize on the new insights that are now possible into consumer shopping habits and behaviour. These insights will come from new data sources, especially data obtained from loyalty cards and shopper research. Leadership advantages in the use of new tools for analysing these data, such as shopper segmentation tools, and for collecting these data, such as in-store kiosks, intelligent shopping carts and in-home scanners, will provide the foundation for unlocking these powerful new insights into shopper behaviour. These insights will provide the information needed to influence shopper behaviour at the point of maximum impact – at the point-of-purchase decision making. This is the essence of shopper marketing.

However, there are some unique forces also driving the industry into shopper marketing. Most notable are the significant changes occurring in the mix of media being used for shopping decisions. Much has been written in recent years about the changes in the information sources used for shopping. There has been a decline in the use of traditional media, such as TV and magazines, and a growth in the use of new shopping media, including the internet, mobile media such as mobile phones, and in-store media, such as in-store TV, kiosks, digital signing, and shopping cart screens. These new shopping media have made the store a marketing medium such as has never before been possible. They enable selling messages to be effectively and efficiently communicated to consumers closer to, or actually at, the very moment of the purchase decision. In combination, these trends have paved the way for the opportunity for a go-to-market strategy based on the platform of shopper marketing. This strategy is enabled by two capabilities: first, the ability to obtain new insights into shopper behaviour and, second, the ability to reach shoppers with targeted communication at the point-of-purchase decision making (the 'moment of truth').

The widespread use of category management over the last 20 years provided the first consumer-based common platform for retailer and manufacturer collaboration in retail-level marketing. Shopper marketing is firmly based on the foundation created by category management. Its focus is on marketing category and brand programmes to the shopper in the store. As a reflection of the close connection between category management and shopper marketing, the 'next generation' of category management best practices is being titled 'shopper and category development' (Harris and Clutts, 2008). It represents the updating of the original 1995 ECR best practices category management report (Efficient consumer response, 1995) to reflect the new opportunities now available for shopper marketing. The new report is being published by The Food Marketing Institute in late 2009. Shopper marketing is the next wave in the evolution of retail marketing practices. It has been shaped and its foundation for success has been created by the practices of the wave that preceded it – category management.

References

Efficient consumer response joint industry project (1995) Category management report

Harris, B (1989) Merchandising management for the 1990s, CIES 39th international conference

Harris, B and Clutts, J (2008) Shopper and category development – the next generation of best practices category management, Food Marketing Institute conference

6 Illogic inside the mind of the shopper

Michael Sansolo

Michael Sansolo, a former senior officer of the Food Marketing Institute (FMI) and editor of *Progressive Grocer*, is an independent consultant in the United States. The FMI conducts programmes in public affairs, food safety, research, education and industry relations on behalf of its 1,500 member companies – food retailers and wholesalers.

If shoppers were logical, simple beings, then understanding them and marketing ·to them would be incredibly simple. In reality, they are complex, illogical and increasingly and frequently contradictory, which makes the process of understanding them more challenging than ever.

Consider, for example, a small story from one US retailer. Each week this supermarket retailer would offer a discount on gasoline prices to customers. One day as he visited the line of drivers and cars waiting to fill up he noticed something odd. Many of the drivers sat in their cars drinking cups of coffee from Starbucks. The paradox was simple: why was it that the shopper who would pay extra money for a cup of coffee from Starbucks (there are less expensive options) would then wait in line to save a few pennies per gallon for gasoline? Why did the same shopper indulge for one liquid while economizing for a second?

Now, obviously the trade-off between coffee and gasoline isn't a perfect example, as one is consumed and the other placed in a car. All but high-performance drivers rarely worry about how their vehicle is enjoying its fuel. We don't feel the same way about coffee.

But the example is far from limited to that. Why does the same shopper gladly buy a lesser brand of one item in the store while remaining incredibly loyal to another? Why does a time-pressed shopper hoping to save time at every step willingly spend extra time on an indulgence like a manicure, which certainly takes extra time and money?

The North American Coca-Cola Retailing Research Council pondered this matter in a recent study called 'The world according to shoppers'. (The study, along with all studies from the various councils, can be found at www.ccrrc.org.) The study's retail guides – from both the United States and Canada – wondered if it would be possible to peer into the mind of a shopper to understand the different moods or mindsets that seem to drive different decisions, different trips and different purchases.

Shopper-driving forces

Using materials and research from NFO Worldwide, the council offered a very unusual idea on shopper behaviour. Shoppers are essentially driven by four key concerns, and each shopper might find a different mix of these concerns guiding decisions depending on the shopping trip, the item to be bought or even the shopper's mood. In no particular order, the four drivers are: time, money, family and personal matters. Time is the pressure of balancing life in a modern society where both mother and father (or frequently a single parent or adult living alone) work and try to run the home. Money is the matter of the budget and making certain that the family can afford what it buys, but also buys what it needs. Family concerns could include the budget, but will also include health and wellness, the enjoyment of every family member and the differing needs of each individual. And personal matters are about what the shopper may do for himself or herself, whether it's that manicure or buying a new and rarely needed set of golf clubs.

The challenge is that seldom does one mood completely dominate. For instance, a financially pressed shopper looking to balance the budget might have money issues weighing heavily on his or her mind, yet must also balance the needs of family and the pressures of time. Time poverty, of course, affects the well off and the struggling. What's more, even well-off shoppers might frequently decide to shop for bargains of specific items, as even they can be careful with money and sometimes just live for the thrill of the hunt. (Visit a Costco store and examine the quality of vehicles in the parking lot and you'll quickly realize it isn't a low-income crowd inside the warehouse.)

Types of shoppers

To provide a better handle on this complexity, the council created a series of personality mindsets that seem to define the moods better. Let's examine each in brief.

The first is the keeper, the person who takes the responsibility of providing for the household through food shopping. These people enjoy shopping and enjoy their responsibility.

In contrast, the second is the quartermaster, who views the task of grocery shopping as a chore and a disliked chore at that. Although the first two have similar motivations, they behave very differently in the store. The keeper is far easier to satisfy because he or she is prone to like the entire experience.

Third is the banker, a budget-minded shopper who knows the family must be fed on a specific budget. This shopper loves to find bargains, and loyalty can be won with great pricing.

The fourth is the seeker, a shopper with a very different agenda. This shopper is looking for new ideas, new tastes and new products. For this group, shopping is a journey of discovery, and this provides an opportunity to sell and delight with new products in all product categories.

Shoppers with our fifth mindset could not be more different. This shopper is desperate, needing a specific item immediately. If you don't have that specific item, this shopper can be lost, certainly for a specific trip.

Sixth comes the reluctant shopper. He or she does the shopping, but wishes for a new way. If reluctant shoppers could hire someone to do the task they would. This shopper dislikes the trip and wants it over quickly.

Price is the sole priority of the bargain hunter. This shopper is on a price mission and will do everything to cut costs, including moving between stores and specials at will. This shopper has a limited range of products on the list, and the prices on those products are the most important attraction in the store.

Our eighth shopper is the courier, doing small grab-and-go trips. In fact, many shoppers become this shopper during the week, when they are running those fill-in trips that dominate the aisles in between the major stocking-up trips. The courier has a limited shopping list and is looking for a combination of speed and price to help.

Last comes our hungry shopper, whose goal is a specific item for an immediate need. This might be a single health item, an immediate meal or even cigarettes. This is a very focused shopping trip.

Targeting consumer segments

In evaluating these shopper mindsets, the marketer has to ask some very pointed questions and consider honestly market realities. First, is the market you are chasing the correct one for your location? Easy examples would be the folly of placing a store built for discovery shoppers in a low-income, working-class neighbourhood. While the shoppers might want that experience, it's unlikely they would find it helpful to their problems. In reverse, a price-only Aldi isn't likely to pop up anytime soon in Beverly Hills. The store could be fabulous, but the shopper base would be wrong.

But the market isn't the only determinant. Marketers also have to consider the competition and honestly assess their strengths and weaknesses against those competitors. If you want to go after the price-oriented shopper, are you in a market where you can succeed or are you simply a second player? It's a very hard assessment to take on, but an essential one.

The justification for these targeted strategies comes across clearly. Survey work completed by NFO for the project revealed the power of formats that are clearly focused and targeted at specific consumer segments (see Figures 6.1 and 6.2). Although the shopping experience might be very different at Whole Foods and at Aldi, the bottom line is that shoppers rate stores much higher when they clearly understand the selling proposition and feel their needs are met satisfactorily.

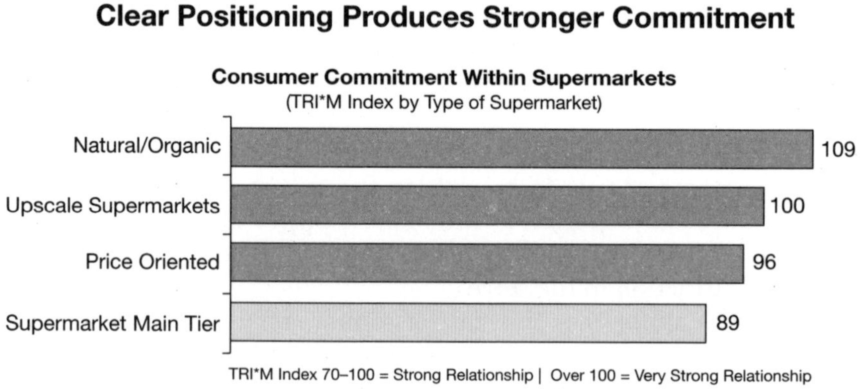

Clear Positioning Produces Stronger Commitment

Consumer Commitment Within Supermarkets
(TRI*M Index by Type of Supermarket)

Type	Index
Natural/Organic	109
Upscale Supermarkets	100
Price Oriented	96
Supermarket Main Tier	89

TRI*M Index 70–100 = Strong Relationship | Over 100 = Very Strong Relationship

Figure 6.1 Clear positioning produces stronger commitment

Supermarkets Are Facing Strong Competition

Consumer Commitment Across Competition
(TRI*M Index, by Channel)

Channel	Index
Limited Assortment	106
Warehouse Club	101
Dollar	100
Mass Merchandiser	93
Supercenter	93
Total Supermarkets	91
Drug Stores	87
Convenience Stores	80

TRI*M Index 70–100 = Strong Relationship | Over 100 = Very Strong Relationship

Figure 6.2 Supermarkets are facing strong competition

In contrast, stores with no obvious appeal get the lower satisfaction ratings. (In fairness, though, the ratings given all food stores were actually fairly high on the studies done by NFO. Yet the highest scores were clearly given to targeted formats.)

Sadly, shoppers don't come through the doors bearing these designations on their foreheads. And there is no way of knowing that the family-minded keeper is in a desperate mood and looking for a vastly different experience on Tuesday night from that on Saturday morning. As with all shopper studies, it isn't possible to unlock every secret to marketing with one set of questions or one review of data.

But the overriding messages are clear. Peering inside the mind of the shopper requires careful attention to local marketing and honest appraisals of competition and your own capabilities. And then the entire staff must understand the goals and deliver on them daily. It won't be easy, but customer marketing rarely – if ever – is.

7 For shoppers there's no place like home

Harvey Hartman

Harvey Hartman is an author and business school lecturer, and the founder, chairman and CEO of the Hartman Group. The Hartman Group is a consulting and consumer insights firm specializing in the analysis and interpretation of consumer lifestyles and how these lifestyles affect the purchase and use of health and wellness products and services.

A considerable amount of the explainable variation in shopping behaviour actually has more to do with things happening in the household than it does with things happening in the store. Here's why the home experience matters. Conventional research focuses on things happening in the store and at the shelf to derive shopper insights. These insights are typically the result of telephone survey and focus group consumer research. At best, insights from these techniques are a bit short-sighted for they do not paint the bigger picture of consumer behaviour. To illustrate our point that the customer experience begins at home rather than at the business theatre we offer the following example.

As our cultural anthropologists followed consumers intensely over a several-week period – interviewing them at home and then tagging along on multiple shopping trips – a curious thing happened. We quickly realized that a considerable amount of the explainable variation in shopping behaviour actually had more to do with things happening in the household than it did with things happening in the store.

When a consumer tosses a pack of Gorton's fish sticks in the cart, she may tell you 'I needed fish sticks and these were on sale', as if efficiently satisfying a need. The reality is that this action is shaped by a dynamic set of cultural practices that intersect in the contemporary US household. Why was this consumer shopping? Why Gorton's? Why fish? Why does 'on sale' matter? For whom is the product intended? As we found out, answers to these questions go further toward explaining shopping behaviour than any model based on the in-store experience.

To help better understand the significance of the household with regard to shopping behaviour, consider Heather, a young mother with an infant, and her three-year-old son, Samuel.

Appeasing the picky child

We followed Heather during her weekly shopping trip to Safeway, with Samuel sitting impatiently in the cart. Although armed with a substantial list of over 30 items, Heather was very open to in-store stimuli, as we noticed when she rounded the corner of one aisle, emerging on to the perimeter of the store. As she turned right, a frozen foods perimeter end-cap caught her eye. She grabbed some Gorton's fish sticks (not on her list) and threw them into her cart, quickly adding to us that she is in 'an ongoing effort to find things [Samuel] might like'. She knew Samuel liked this brand of fish sticks and so into the cart went the fish sticks, even though they weren't on her list. Heather mentioned in an earlier in-home interview that she has had to find very special foods to satisfy Samuel's increasingly picky cravings. Fish sticks are just one of a small list of things she has isolated to accomplish this ongoing task.

Our research continues to show that Heather isn't alone in her endless search for products to satisfy picky young eaters. In fact, Heather's behaviour is but one example of a broader cultural approach to dealing with picky children through strategic forms of appeasement that minimize conflict in the home. For these parents, harmony is more important than enforcing dietary discipline and dealing with the rebellion this causes. For many of these households, parents often develop a stock group of foods that they will use to quiet and feed the child, before moving on with their day. Examples of these appeasement foods include fish sticks, hot dogs, chicken nuggets, Cheerios, Hot Pockets, etc. All of these products are easy for young mouths to chew on, are tasty and don't require utensils. Parents use these foods to placate young children between meals or, more importantly, provide an alternative to the parents' meal. Parents who select foods to appease picky children often keep a stock set of these foods on hand, referring to them as their children's food. The children sometimes grow up fondly remembering these foods (and the brands associated with them) as the ultimate in 'comfort food'.

Emerging lessons from the home experience: the genesis of true brand loyalty is often the home

What Heather randomly grabbed off a Safeway end-cap may, if she repeatedly buys it, become a lifelong brand preference for Samuel – a preference whose origin will forever be as hazy for him as his own birth and yet potentially quite strong. This is how many of us have come to orient ourselves toward consumer packaged goods brands such as Coca-Cola, Pepsi and Nabisco: our mother purchased something for us, which we seemed to like, so she kept buying it. The brand descended from the maternal heavens, so to speak, and we grew up thinking it was simply the brand all right-thinking people purchase and use. In this, what begins as the expression of a simple taste preference (our mother buys Oreos because, as far as she can tell, we seem to prefer them to Vanilla Wafers) is imbued with a moral character (we purchase Oreos because that's what our mother did – it's simply the way things are done). Although many new grocery brands have entered the scene since our birth, the enduring power of these traditional brands still maintains a compelling and often moralistic grip – and, we might add, has everything to do with the shopping experience or the experience of shopping.

Home experiences generate cultural tasks, not need states

Appeasing a picky child does not fit neatly into a model of need states. After all, there are many ways to deal with picky children (a combination of discipline and/or tough love was in vogue 30 years ago); appeasing them with their preferred food is merely one strategy that appears to have achieved some measure of current cultural legitimacy. Moreover, appeasing the child is not a shopper need; it is an arbitrary task consumers have assigned to themselves based on the combined influence of their at-home experience and larger cultural trends from beyond the home.

The Hartman Group's integrated approach to shopper insights has allowed them to identify five commonly held beliefs of shopping behaviour that fail to materialize beyond mere assumptions.

Here is the Hartman Group's perspective on these five myths of shopping behaviour:

 Myth: Brand loyalty drives shopping behaviour.
Reality: Brand loyalty falls by the wayside for the sake of getting things done: 'What can I get at this store to accomplish x, y and z tasks?'

 Myth: Retail environments build brand loyalty.
Reality: Retail is not the site for brand building for traditional CPG brands. For these established brands, loyalty is formed mainly in the household.

 Myth: Behavioural scripts drive shopping behaviour.
Reality: Because most FDM retail shopping is less about identity cues, behavioural scripts take a back seat to cultural occasions.

 Myth: Shopping behaviour is about fulfilling fixed needs.
Reality: Cultural occasions drive shopping behaviour. Products and brands are tools to complete occasion-specific tasks, not drivers of shopping experience.

 Myth: Shopping behaviour varies by category.
Reality: Consumers shop differently depending upon distinctions of packaged vs fresh, rather than the structure of common grocery and drug categories.

Source: Hartman Group (2005) *Shopper Insights: How cultural occasions frame the consumer experience*, Hartman Group, Bellevue, WA

Figure 7.1 Five common myths of shopping behaviour

For example, one of many approaches to dealing with the picky eater is to hunt for pre-approved food categories that head off confrontation in the kitchen. Parents who opt for this approach (and there are millions of them out there) participate in a culturally shaped approach to parenting young children, one reinforced within their own social networks (where they share knowledge about what kinds of foods and products work in appeasing their own children). These parents are often those who allow their children to develop their own taste preferences early on in life. They often, for example, ask their children while in the store, 'Would you like this?' In fact, this approach to feeding young children is so common now that many people find it difficult to remember a different one. And it is an approach to parenting that finds constant support within social networks (ie at the coffee shop, at the gym, at the PTA meeting and at the book club).

As you can see, experiences in the home are constantly generating new tasks to be accomplished. These tasks aren't 'needs' so much as shifting orientations that simply feel necessary. It is these tasks that then send people out to shop. In other words, it is the at-home experience that, in large part, fuels the dynamic engine of cultural orientations to products, brands and the overall shopping experience. Rather than shopping robotically for brand 'x' or product 'y', even loyal purchasers make decisions that derive their power from positively reinforced at-home consumption experiences.

This framework of thinking has far-reaching implications beyond the retail food arena, as it is not limited to any industry, channel or manufacturer. The potential drivers of shopping behaviour reside within the household and are intrinsically linked to brand building in the at-home experience. Our ongoing research continues to investigate and measure the role of:

- household social structures on shopping behaviour;
- social networks external to the home influencing consumption habits within the home;
- consumption occasions within the home;
- taste and preference formation within the home on future shopping behaviour;
- product design with regard to storage and consumption within the household;
- household orientations to household finance on consumption;
- orientations (however fragmented) towards food, personal care and health.

8 Shopper mega-trends: health, wellness and the environment

Sara Lubbers

Sara Lubbers is the director of insights and research for Malone Advertising. She is responsible for interpreting data and translating research findings into usable insights. Malone Advertising is a retail specialist agency that has been connecting with shoppers along their path to purchase for 65 years.

Health and wellness (H&W) and being 'green' are two of the most talked-about trends among marketers today. Marketers have an opportunity to capitalize on compelling, motivating messages if they can identify what shoppers want to know and how they want to receive communication.

Methodology

The following insights are based on an ongoing series of shopper studies called ShopperSight – a collaboration between Malone Advertising and MVI. The studies are fielded online and designed to obtain account-specific shopper insights for top grocery, drug and mass retailers. The studies are fielded online via SONAR/Consumer Link, which is a panel of 70,000 active panellists. At least 300 samples are obtained per retailer, with a total sample size of about 2,500 per study.

High interest

Not only are the vast majority of shoppers interested in health and wellness and being green to at least some degree, but they have also indicated that they want help in 'being good'. They want help eating healthily; they want help going green; they want help planning nutritious meals for their family; etc.

Shoppers do not think these trends are merely marketing hype – for example, in the green/sustainability study only 2 in 10 respondents agreed that 'the "green" issue is just a way to sell more products'.

All are one

Being green, organics, health and wellness – we're seeing that, in the consumer's mind, all these concepts run together, whereas retailers and manufacturers tend to compartmentalize them. Merging these concepts into one lifestyle-oriented platform plays out in many ways:

- *No segregation:* isolating natural and organic products in a separate section of the store doesn't seem to make sense with how consumers shop. Shoppers want to see H&W and green information right at the shelf where they're making choices, and be able to compare products side by side. As health and wellness and being green are mainstream to consumers, it makes sense to have the products integrated. We've seen retailers take a number of different approaches here, from separate naturals sections of the store and circulars, to having greener products pointed out with signage or a bump-out in the aisle, to having the products completely integrated with conventional products with only the packaging indicating their green benefits.
- *One voice, many messages:* marketers can communicate health benefits, sustainability benefits, and organics with the same messaging platform. This consistency would benefit shoppers by allowing them quickly to identify the characteristics of the products they're considering and make informed choices. It also offers the likelihood of potentially up-selling shoppers if the communicated benefits offer compelling value. A retailer that has applied this principle visibly in-store is likely to target consumers with its 'long live healthy' campaign, and a 'long live Earth friendly' message living under that same umbrella.

Cross-fertilization

Because health and wellness and being green are linked in consumers' minds, some interesting promotional opportunities emerge – for example, pairing vitamins with an organic beauty care line with a 'be good to your skin, be good to the earth' message.

Shoppers have good intentions, but fall short in the follow-through. With both green living and H&W, there's huge awareness but less action. Price and convenience are the two big stumbling blocks in both cases – especially for busy parents.

Use multiple benefits

Because price is a major roadblock for both health-oriented and environmentally friendly products, shoppers are looking for additional benefits to help them justify the additional expense – for example, healthy and convenient; green and saves money long-term; healthy and superior taste; green and effective; etc.

Although 68% of consumers say it's important to eat healthily every day, a number of shoppers feel that it is difficult to find convenient, healthy food in stores.

Figure 8.1 Parents mean well, but they don't plan well

Credibility is key

Shoppers have high expectations for their retailers in terms of green living and H&W. With H&W, the pharmacy seems to be a linchpin for credibility. Especially in H&W, but even in green living, the drug channel is seen as a credible source of information. For green living, third-party validation is another key to credibility.

Publix, a grocery retailer in the southern United States, has done a tremendous job of establishing credibility in both green living and health and wellness among shoppers. It publishes a magazine devoted to healthy and sustainable living, it has an extensive literature programme with green living and wellness information, and its efforts have paid huge dividends in shopper confidence.

On the other hand, Wal-Mart has made enormous effort to increase its sustainability in terms of improving energy efficiency, streamlining logistics, and encouraging manufacturers to do the same. However, these efforts have not translated into shopper satisfaction or confidence in this area – and this can be linked to a lack of visibility at the store level.

Set a standard

With both green and health and wellness messages, consumers are faced with a variety of statements with no set standard to refer to (except in the case of organics, where there's still an information gap). There's an opportunity for retailers to create a scorecard ranking system based on sustainability of products, eco-friendly packaging and manufacturing processes, health and wellness attributes, portion control, etc.

Overall, shoppers look to product packaging for green information when shopping.

Shoppers seem to have fine-tuned vision when seeking out green information – they go directly to the source (package) versus looking for bigger-picture clues (store section, shelf or display).

Figure 8.2 Green information on the packaging

Instant gratification

For both health and wellness and green living, shoppers want to see product attributes right on the product as they're making final purchase selections. The further communication is from the point of sale, the less interested shoppers are in that vehicle. The exception may be getting information online, which was the most favoured out-of-store communication method for product health and sustainability information.

Tracking trends

Investing in shopper insights relative to specific categories, trip types, and target audiences requires incredible investment and microscopic attention to detail. However, as a more detailed picture emerges, there are also large, overarching themes that become apparent. Recognizing the patterns out of the detail, and watching the trends even among trends, can help marketers make smart, predictive decisions ahead of the curve.

9 Understanding shoppers' complex decisions

Gerardine Padbury

Gerardine Padbury is a senior consumer analyst for IGD, where she conducts regular consumer and shopper research. IGD provides research, information and education for the food and grocery industry.

Complex shopper decisions

Gone are the days when food and drink solely satisfied a purely physiological need. Today, they are something that help us define who we are as individuals, meeting our social and aspirational needs. Whether it's a demand for healthier products for our families, foods that adhere to our ethical and environmental values, or foods that allow us to indulge ourselves, the decisions we're making about what we buy, when and where have never been more complex. This is, at least in part, because we have never received so much communication about our food and drink products, to the extent that sometimes it can be overwhelming, causing confusion and dissatisfaction. With so much information and so much choice we are faced with complex decisions, which will involve a certain degree of trading off. How consumers react when faced with difficult trade-offs depends on what is most important to them, which in turn varies by category, product and occasion. External forces affecting shopper choices include the changing world economy, population and cultural shifts, climate change, growing obesity levels and concern for health, and an increasing awareness about how food is produced.

Values and value

Price, while still important, is balanced against a number of other factors that constitute value for the shopper. These include the quality of the ingredients, the health benefits and the social and environmental impact of production.

Respondents in IGD focus groups often mention the fact that they will not choose products on price alone, as buying the cheapest products is often considered to be a false economy. Getting assurances that products will be fit for purpose and meet the requirements of the shopper will be achieved by shoppers buying brands that they trust or by checking the contents of the product.

The food industry, and in particular retailers, needs to provide assurances to shoppers that they are getting value for money. This communication is more important from a retail perspective, as price plays a more important role in store choice than it does in product choice. Shoppers trust the price competitiveness of a store for individual items based on their overall price perceptions of that supermarket.

Price continues to be mentioned as a key driver of store choice by almost six in ten of all shoppers (58 per cent). Price as a driver has been in decline in recent years having peaked at 65 per cent in 2006. The latest figures, however, indicate that price is returning to the forefront of shoppers' minds. However, it is still not as strong a driver of store choice as in 2006. We suspect this could be due to the actual or perceived price gap narrowing between retailers.

Health

Stories about the state of the nation's diet and the food industry's role in providing healthy choices are regularly in the news. In recent years IGD has found that shoppers are becoming increasingly aware of the link between diet and health. This trend is likely to continue, influenced by an ageing population concerned about health and well-being and enhanced awareness of nutritional issues. Knowing all of the ingredients in a product has become increasingly important to shoppers over the past five years, with around one in three shoppers (31 per cent) now claiming it as one of the most important drivers of product choice. Only a quarter (24 per cent) mentioned this in 2003.

A growing demand for products that are healthy comes through in the findings of IGD's *Shopper trends 2009 – food shopping in a recession* research. Messages on health appear to be having an impact on shoppers, with many altering their diet and trying to move towards a healthier lifestyle. The success of the five-fruit-and-vegetables-a-day campaign in the UK is clearly demonstrated, with 41 per cent of shoppers indicating they are eating five daily portions of fruit and vegetables as part of a healthy lifestyle. This is compared to 32 per cent in 2006.

For the industry, the pressure to offer a healthy proposition will increase in line with growing media attention and the need to act responsibly towards shoppers. Key to being successful will include how health benefits are communicated in an environment where news headlines often provide conflicting and confusing messages.

Provenance

Shoppers have more choice than ever before when it comes to choosing local, regional, national or international food and grocery products. With increased migration throughout the world, international food aisles have expanded to meet the demands of new culturally and ethnically diverse populations.

In the United Kingdom there has been increased popularity in purchasing local and regional food from a variety of channels, ranging from farmers' markets to supermarkets. However, with broader concerns about climate change being high on the consumer agenda, shoppers may increasingly question how far their food has travelled and how it has been produced.

Knowing where food has come from is more important to shoppers now than it was in 2003. This is demonstrated by the following findings from IGD shopper research:

- Almost one-quarter of shoppers (23 per cent) said that knowing which country the product has come from is an important consideration in choosing products. This was mentioned by 15 per cent of respondents in 2003.
- Over one-quarter (27 per cent) of shoppers said that they had specifically bought products in the last month that had been produced in the area where they live (up from 15 per cent in 2003).
- A fifth (20 per cent) of shoppers in 2009, compared to 9 per cent in 2003, indicated that the distance the food has travelled is a production concern for them.

Some shoppers want to bring fairness to farmers and producers, at home and abroad. They are also increasingly hungry for knowledge about where their food has come from, how sustainable it is and the implications for future generations. This also is reflected in the growing interest in ethical and environmental issues.

Ethics and the environment

Over the years to come, consumers will be making some tough decisions regarding food ethics, seeking to reconcile their own preferences with their wider responsibilities. However, while some shoppers might aspire to buying foods that will make a difference to the wider environment, they may not always be able to afford to buy what they would like to. Ethical and environmental issues are high on the agenda for the industry and for shoppers alike. While British shoppers would like to see the industry improve performance in areas such as supporting British producers and reducing packaging, they are increasingly aware of the wider consequences of their purchasing decisions and recognize that they too can make a difference.

When IGD researched this issue in its *Ethical shopping – are shoppers turning green?* report, it was found that shoppers in the UK rely on a number of guiding principles to help them navigate the growing complexity of trade-offs associated with shopping decisions.

Where once ethical products were packaged in a subdued manner, if they made it on to the shelf at all, the growing market means it is critical to address underlying consumer needs when communicating the benefits of an ethical brand or product.

The paradox of packaging

In 2004, a US psychology professor, Barry Schwartz, wrote *The Paradox of Choice*, which suggests that increased choice, rather than increasing personal satisfaction and freedom, can actually have a detrimental effect on our emotional well-being. Considering the many demands made by shoppers today it would appear that there is a need for choice to meet these growing demands. Also in shopper research by IGD in 2007, shoppers indicated that they are generally satisfied with the choice offered to them. While each individual may not require the vast array of choice available, it was recognized by shoppers that each person will have different requirements. For information too, most shoppers will tend to see only what is personally relevant, meaningful and valued by themselves, and consequently they filter out information that is not specifically relevant to them or their family.

However, there is a real danger of information overload if the trend of adding more information to labels continues unabated. A new paradox now exists as ethical and environmental issues grow in importance. Shoppers have indicated that they would most like to get nutritional, environmental and ethical information on the front of pack or back of pack, yet at the same time they want to see packaging reduced. Providing all the information that shoppers require in an easily accessible place while providing environmentally friendly packaging will be a key challenge for the food industry in the future. What is clear is that the explosion in product information demanded by consumers, and the diverse information needs of shoppers, requires discipline, coordination and management of product data throughout the supply chain from ingredients to end product and packaging. Manufacturers and retailers would be advised to be prepared for consumers' increased thirst for product knowledge.

10 The three shopping currencies

Herb Sorensen

Dr Herb Sorensen is global scientific director of shopper insights at TNS Sorensen. Since the late 1970s his market research has focused on shoppers at their points of purchase. TNS Sorensen, the in-store research company®, captures shopper behaviour, motivations and perceptions at the point of purchase.

Retailing is a relationship business

Retailing is all about bringing people together with the things they want and need. It has always been at the cutting edge of social evolution – and always will be. To really understand retailing, it is helpful to think of it in relationship terms – that is, to think in terms of the variety of relationships that most seriously affect retail. These are illustrated in Figure 10.1.

For much of retail, the dominant relationship driving the practice is that between the retailer and the product suppliers. This is especially true in a self-service world where the retailer's primary responsibility is to provide a store stocked with merchandise, and the primary responsibility of the supplier is just that – to supply the merchandise with which the store is stocked. This leaves self-service customers to self-build their own relationships primarily with the store and the product within, the retailer and supplier being remote parties of little interest or involvement with the customer.

This is the stark reality that drives a good deal of retailing. It is not that either retailers or suppliers seek to have this relationship with

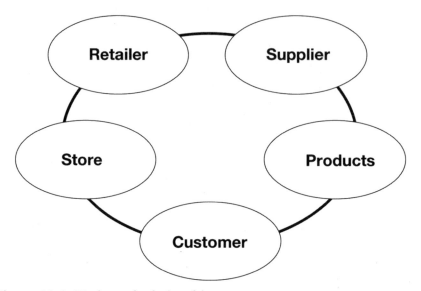

Figure 10.1 Variety of relationships

shoppers, but their own mutual relationship tends to cause relationships to the shoppers to pale in significance, and to remain somewhat distant, by comparison. This is the reality of self-service.

The 'give-gets' of the shopper in the store

The purpose of this chapter is to examine in more detail the relationships that shoppers develop with the store and the products. For this purpose, we first consider the store in an economic/engineering model of inputs and outputs, relative to the shopper. As the chapter title suggests, there are three shopper inputs to the store: what we refer to as the three currencies. And then there are the two basic outputs of the store. These five are the 'give-gets' between the shopper and the store. The shopper gives money, time and angst and gets items and satisfaction.

The advent of electronic checkout scanners in the 1970s opened the way for massive and relatively accurate measurement of the money and items, the two most obvious of the shopper's give-gets. In fact, two of the largest research organizations in the world, IRI and Nielsen, are founded on the business of compiling the counts of these two variables and metering them out to both retailers and suppliers, for a healthy stream of profits.

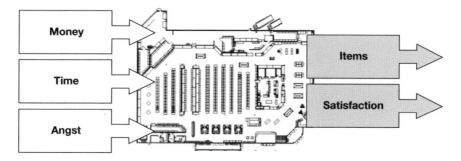

Figure 10.2 'Give-gets' between the shopper and the store

However, it is noteworthy that, for very many years, great numbers of retailers used scanner data for little more than totalling up the shopper's payment at the checkout, and for inventory control: monitoring the flow of goods through the store. It is especially significant that these data are summed up at the store level and compiled on a weekly basis. Weekly totals are hardly the kind of detail that might be required in terms of understanding actual shopper behaviour in the store. That is, these are rough measures, albeit in truckload quantities, that measure what goes in and out of the store on a weekly basis, but say very little about the process of what happens inside the store.

This is not to dismiss the value of this input–output information, especially on a competitive basis – channels, chains, categories, brands and even individual items. This tremendous value, particularly to the supplier, accounts for massive attention to every slight fluctuation in these numbers. But, again, those fluctuations are not necessarily very revealing about the causes.

Relating single-item purchases to individual shoppers

In the past decade, there has been tremendous growth in the recognition of the value of transaction data, when associated with specific shoppers, through shopper loyalty card information, rather than weekly purchases of the non-discriminated crowd. In fact, what was at the time a very small consultancy, dunnhumby, looking at the purchases of individual shoppers, linked to their demographic and other characteristics, assisted Tesco's move up to the position of third largest retailer globally.

The data for this purpose do not even exist in the weekly roll-ups that are provided by Nielsen and IRI. It is not just shopper identity that is required, but the detailed log of every single shopper's every single shopping trip and every single item purchased on those shopping trips – or at least a very large number of them.

However, as salutary as the marriage of transaction log data to demographics and psychographics might be, this is still input–output type data that do not address the actual process within the store. If we look at the outputs from the store, we see that satisfaction is also an output. It is interesting that a wide variety of organizations and methods have focused on determining, in more or less systematic ways, customer satisfaction. All of these programmes can have tremendous value in providing a view of shoppers' state of mind as they exit the store or, more often, some time after their store experience.

The point here is that, again, this is an output measure, not a process measure. Thus all three of the common measures of the store in relationship to the shopper are inputs and outputs to the store that can, at best, provide only inferential information about what is happening within the store. In fact, we submit that, given the lack of direct measurement of behaviour within the store, it is fair to describe the store as more or less a black box to all three of the major parties to the store: shopper, supplier and retailer. A good deal more objective evidence in support of this assertion could be offered, but that is not the purpose of this chapter. Rather, we seek to shine a bit more light on the store by showing the importance of the other two inputs, time and angst, and outline metrics and the application to retail profits, which should be of great interest.

Time as the measure of shopping

If counts of items and the money associated with their purchase are the two most crucial measures of outputs and inputs, then time is the most crucial process measure. That is, money and items measure purchasing, but it is time that measures shopping. This may not seem readily apparent, but in our own work of tracking millions of shopping trips on a second-by-second basis it has become apparent that it is time that distinguishes a visitor from a shopper.

Think about it: if you are a supplier that wishes to move merchandise through a retail establishment, it isn't having shoppers in the store that brings you sales; it is having shoppers in the aisle or location where your merchandise is. More than this, it is not just shoppers who are hurrying past your location on their way to somewhere else, but shoppers who are spending at least a modicum of time considering your, and your competitors', offerings. Traffic in itself never buys anything; it is traffic investing time that becomes shopping. Figure 10.3 shows the relationship between the share of baskets with a breakfast cereal purchase and the share of baskets that pass, that is, traffic past the breakfast cereal. Simply, there is no relationship between the two because in most stores the traffic past cereal has little to do with interest in cereal: that aisle is simply a convenient (or not) aisle to somewhere shoppers want to get to. (On this point, a study at the Wharton school confirmed that a high percentage of individual shoppers' time is spent transiting about the store, not directly involved in acquiring merchandise.)

The important takeaway here is that time is the vital ingredient that converted some share of these visitors into buyers, and it converted to about the same final rate of purchase in all the stores. Clearly we need to understand better the potent power of this second currency, time.

There is a second point here worth noting: although there is certainly variability from store to store in terms of share of baskets purchasing a category – cereal as the example – the reality is that the share of baskets with category purchases is relatively constant across stores. In this case, about 9 per cent of baskets contain a cereal purchase across this series of stores across the United States, across chains. To be sure, some sell more and some sell less, but the relative constancy of category sales is a reflection of the constancy of crowds. Although there will be differences, any 100,000 people will behave pretty much as any

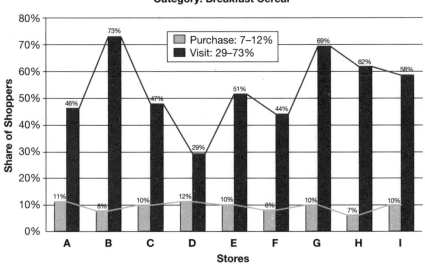

Figure 10.3 Category: breakfast cereal

other 100,000 people will, at least in terms of cereal purchases (and for most other categories, for most of the time).

Time is opportunity to sell

Based on a variety of lines of evidence, it is apparent that it takes about a second for a shopper to actually take note of a stimulus, whether of a package, a product display or some other media. This means that one second of one shopper's time is a pretty good basis for measuring how much shopping is going on. Hence, shopper-seconds are the basic unit of shopping.

Another way to look at the shopper-second is to realize that each second a shopper is in the store is another opportunity to sell the shopper something. This is the key to using time as more than just an input measure. Of course, we could measure how long a shopper is in the store, and count the money the shopper spends, and determine how many seconds it takes for him or her to spend a dollar, pound, euro, baht or whatever. In fact, we can measure all the shopper-seconds from all of the shoppers in the store, and compare that to all the money the store takes in, to determine the efficiency of the retailer's use of the shopper's time, as a store performance measure. Why not?

Retailers commonly compute the turnover of cash per square foot or metre. This is certainly a useful and valid measure of the productivity of the real estate. Why wouldn't we want something to tell us the productivity of shoppers' use of an asset of great value to them? In fact, it is not too great a stretch to say that many retailers know a good deal more about the management of real estate (and inventory) than they do about the management of shoppers. As alluded to earlier, one can succeed in retailing with this situation because it is self-service, and shoppers are expected to manage their own shopping experience.

Participating with the shopper – 'active retailing'

In order to become actively engaged with the shopper, it is necessary to understand how shoppers are spending their time in the store – or perhaps understand where shoppers are spending their time in the store. The reason for this is so that, rather than waiting passively for shoppers to find their way to the merchandise they need, we can actively understand their needs and make relevant offers to them to expedite their purchases. This is a crucial concept because, instead of frustrating shoppers by trying to 'build basket size' by holding them in the store longer, hoping they will buy something more, we will 'build basket size' by getting more merchandise into their baskets more quickly. The simple fact is that holding them in the store longer, in the long run, will mean that they won't be coming here so often, because, in the long run, whether they put words to it or not, they will come to realize that you are not being as helpful as your competition.

So let's consider a not unusual shopping trip, shown in Figure 10.4, that begins with the shopper coming through the door, in this case on the right side of the store.

There is very little opportunity to sell to the shopper in the darker areas, with much better opportunities in the lighter areas, where shoppers spend an average to a much more than average amount of time. It has taken me years to stop thinking about how to get shoppers to those darker areas and instead to focus on how to sell them more in the lighter areas, but this is the very essence of active retailing – focus on the shopper, rather than trying to get the shopper to focus on the merchandise.

Here we see a great amount of shoppers' time just inside the entrance, with substantial numbers of shoppers making their way – in a counter-clockwise fashion – around the perimeter of the store. When

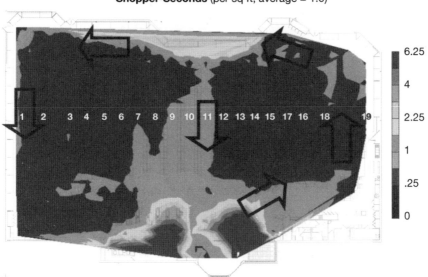

Figure 10.4 Shopper-seconds

they get to the back of the store, they are ready to leave, and begin to move through the broad back aisle across the store.

Notice what happens next. When they look down the first aisles, on their left, what do they see? They see the produce and customer service areas where they started their trip (see Figure 10.5).

But, as they continue across the store, they eventually come to an aisle where the view at the front is not merchandise (see Figure 10.6).

And so, you see, the first heavily travelled aisle, from the back of the store to the front, is the first aisle that leads to the checkout stands and the exit. This is a pattern that is repeated in store after store. In fact, in general, as shoppers get nearer and nearer the checkout, they shop faster and faster – using most of their 'leisure' at the beginning of the trip. The phenomenon is so pronounced and regular that we refer to it as 'the checkout magnet'.

Figure 10.5 Supermarket shelves

Figure 10.6 Supermarket checkout

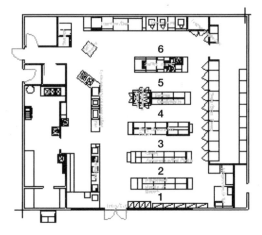

Convenience – 2,100 sq ft

Figure 10.7 Convenience store

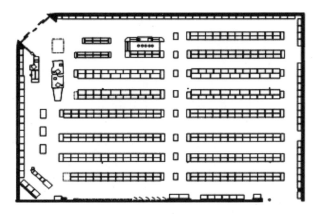

Drugstore – 12,000 sq ft

Figure 10.8 Drugstore

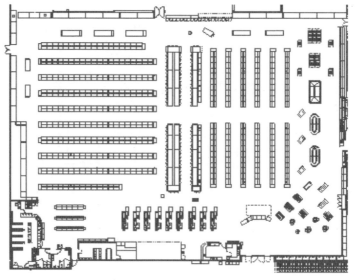

Supermarket – 60,000 sq ft

Figure 10.9 Supermarket

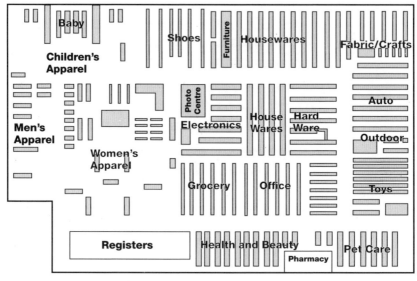

Mass Merchandising – 120,000 sq ft

Figure 10.10 Mass merchandising store

Understanding shopper behaviour vis-à-vis understanding products

But there is a very important point: this behaviour is not driven by the location or arrangement of merchandise! In fact, a very large share of shopper behaviour in the store is not driven by the merchandise. As we noted before, only a minority of the shopper's time is actually spent in the direct acquisition of merchandise. The role of active retailing is to identify this non-economically productive time and to do more selling during that time. Simply attempting to increase shopper time in the store has counterproductively led to fewer shopping trips, of shorter duration.

Another way to look at this is, instead of trying to lure shoppers to where they are not, instead learn where they are (and where they are going) and merchandise to that. But, of course, this active retailing will begin with knowledge of just where the shoppers are spending their time. It is shopper knowledge rather than product knowledge, the latter being the speciality of most retailers and their suppliers.

Lest it be thought that this is only about supermarkets, these principles have been validated across a great number of retail establishments, from full-size shopping malls to closet-like convenience stores (see Figures 10.7 to 10.10). Using shopper-seconds as a standard metric brings retailers into close alignment with the second currency of great concern to shoppers. We now turn our attention to the third currency: angst.

Angst: a vague, unpleasant emotion

The third currency of shopping is easy to understand, but difficult to measure. It's a psychic, emotional deficit that can involve anything from a long checkout line to an out-of-stock item. Although it may be difficult to measure, this doesn't mean that the effects are slight or inconsequential. For our discussion here we want to focus on two major drivers of angst, both of which are related to the matter of choice.

In his book *The Paradox of Choice*, Barry Schwartz describes an experiment involving product demonstrations at matched stores:

> In one condition of the study, 6 varieties of the jam were available for tasting. In another, 24 varieties were available. In either case, the entire set of 24 varieties was available for purchase. The large array of jams attracted more people to the table than the small array, though in both cases people tasted about the same number of jams on average.

When it came to buying, however, a huge difference became evident. Thirty percent of the people exposed to the small array of jams actually bought a jar; only 3 percent of those exposed to the large array of jams did so.

(Schwartz, 2004: 19–20)

As Dr Schwartz notes: 'A large array of options may discourage consumers because it forces an increase in the effort that goes into making a decision. So consumers decide not to decide, and don't buy the product.' In this case, fewer choices led to 10 times as much purchase!

Generally speaking, people fall into one of two camps on this issue, described as 'satisficers' and 'optimizers'. When shopping, for the satisficer there is an inner standard, a hurdle, that any product meeting or exceeding the standard will be accepted as satisfying, and no further consideration is needed. However, many shoppers are optimizers, for whom no level is satisfying if there may be a better option. And just what is 'better' can be a matter of complexity, involving personal tastes, price, objective quality, image, etc. But the bottom line is that more choices may create massive angst, leading to non-purchase, even in the face of considerable motivation to buy.

Choices, choices, choices

Putting this into market context for fast-moving consumer goods, a retailer begins inventory choices from more than a million individual items (stock keeping units – SKUs) in various supplier warehouses. From these, something like 30,000–40,000 items are selected to offer to shoppers in a supermarket. However, individual households purchase only 300–400 different items in an entire year! And only about half of those are purchased regularly, month in and month out, throughout the year.

If these shopper purchases are reduced to individual shopping trips, the picture becomes even more shocking and angst producing (for the shopper). Half of all supermarket shopping trips result in five or fewer items purchased! These numbers are as solid and factual as anything could be in retail, having been validated (so far) on every continent except Africa and Antarctica.

The fact is that one single item is the most common purchase, as seen in the transaction logs of major retailers around the world. And yet retailers are often focused on 'the stock-up shopper'. It is true that those baskets with 20 or more items have a lot of economic value to the retailer, but what about the people bringing those baskets to the check-

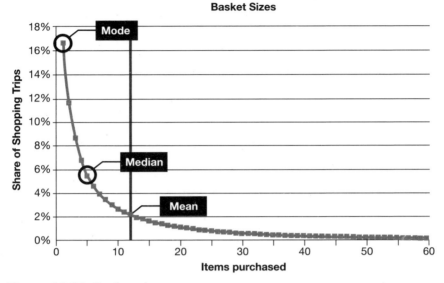

Figure 10.11 Basket sizes

outs? These very same 'stock-up shoppers' are virtually ignored, strategically, for the vast majority of their trips to the store, during which they acquire one or a few items. They are still 'stock-up shoppers', just on a different trip. Is it any wonder that an entire industry grew up to service the quick-trippers? Convenience stores are an illustration of what happens to 'stock-up shoppers' when they are not welcomed in their usual establishments for those quick and fill-in trips.

But how about stock-up shoppers when they are on a stock-up trip? Supermarkets in the United States typically have sales of $10 million to $20 million per year. The very good stores may hit $30 million to $50 million per year. However, one chain manages stores that regularly push $100 million per year – that is, they sell twice to 10 times the sales of the competition, per store. Management of those stores cite premium customer service as a major factor in their success. It is certainly a factor, but is unlikely to account for the performance of the stores. There are three other factors, two of which relate to choice, that need to be considered. The first of these is that the store offers shoppers only 2,000 items from which to make their selections. Is that adequate to generate 10 times more sales than competitive stores? Well, it constitutes about 10 times more items than the typical household will regularly buy. Think of it this way: 2,000 items, properly selected, can provide a shopper with 10 options for every item he or she typically purchases. Even given the diversity of tastes in a major metropolitan area, there are probably not many people who wouldn't find their own needs met at a Stew Leonard's (the chain cited here). More importantly, think of the massive reduction in angst when shoppers do not have to wade through those other 35,000 items to find just those they need. So Stew Leonard's makes massive choices for shoppers, and they reward the reduction in angst with massive purchases.

The second choice issue addressed at Stew Leonard's relates to navigation of the store. There is no question that part of the angst issue in most stores is where the various items are. This problem is greatly alleviated at Stew Leonard's by eliminating navigation! How is this done? Simple: there is only one aisle in the store! That is, the store mostly consists of one wide aisle that snakes its way through the store, so that, as shoppers traverse this one aisle, they are exposed to all the merchandise in the store. Of course, that's only 2,000 items (plenty), but it's all there, everything the typical household needs – and 10 times more. This means shoppers don't have to spend any time wondering where this or that is, but simply devote 100 per cent of their time to assessing the moveable feast that passes effortlessly past them as they move along with the comforting crowd of fellow shoppers, all enjoying the same angst-limited shopping trip.

The third factor (beyond customer service) is the very large amount of fresh content. In fact, at its core, Stew Leonard's is, as advertised, a dairy store, and the business has its roots in that business. So, even though it is a full grocery business, it does have a strong focus on fresh merchandise.

None of this is intended as a paean to Stew Leonard's, but rather as a focus on the three currencies that the shopper pays in the store: money, time and angst. The key to retailer profits – and massive customer satisfaction to go with massive amounts of merchandise removed from the store – is to deliver those goods with an optimum of time, angst and money. This is the crux of the matter – what is the optimum? The reality is that money, time and angst are themselves interrelated, so there is

Figure 10.12 Supermarket

not a single optimum. To illustrate this point, consider an experience at Campbell's soup years ago, when it was recognized that soup, with all those little cans and large number of varieties, represented some real challenges for shoppers attempting to find the specific item(s) they wanted. So, in a carefully controlled matched-store test, the soup was alphabetized (just as spices are). Sure enough, shoppers could find their targeted variety more readily – reduced angst – but they also bought less soup, presumably because they missed buying impulse varieties they just happened to come across while looking for their target varieties.

This illustrates what we have long observed: any rule of rational retailing can be profitably violated. We could multiply examples of this, but these profitable violations do not invalidate the principles behind the rules, and retailers who understand those principles can measure the impact of this or that retail practice, relative to the rules.

In spite of the extraordinary success of Stew Leonard's, there are valid reasons why the industry hasn't stampeded to that retail model. These reasons include the economics of the retailer–supplier relation, as well as competitive supplier–supplier relations. What is referred to as 'SKU proliferation' is not an altogether irrational free-market response, providing genuine shopper benefits. But there are perhaps many players in the game with little understanding of the costs. It is our goal to shed some light through use of metrics.

A full discussion of current and likely future trends is not practical here, but we do note some strong players taking actions. This is not intended to be a broad survey but just two examples.

HEB's central market in Plano, Texas, appears to incorporate some of the same elements extolled above. These are mostly a serpentine path through a full-sized store, with lots of 'fresh' merchandise. There are currently eight stores, twice as many as Stew Leonard's, but they are backed by a much larger regional chain. Although we are not privy to the economic performance of either chain, the growth of this concept shows a lot of promise.

Tesco's Fresh & Easy in the American South-West clearly targets fresh merchandise, but is also focused on large numbers of quick trips. The navigation angst is minimized by the small stores, and there are only 3,500 items in the stores. However, the stores retain the typical grocery store 'warehouse'-type aisles, albeit with lower shelf height, which gives the store a generally more open atmosphere.

Reference

Schwartz, B (2004) *The Paradox of Choice: Why more is less*, HarperCollins, New York

11 Making your brand part of a shopper solution

Jon Kramer

Jon Kramer is chief marketing officer of Alliance, a division of RockTenn, an in-store marketing solutions provider. Alliance is an in-store marketing solutions provider dedicated to developing both promotional and permanent displays, merchandising systems and packaging programmes, supported by innovative marketing services.

Shopper marketing is the next logical evolution in the relationship between manufacturers and retailers. If looked at from 30,000 feet, it represents the next logical progression from account-specific activities in the 1980s to co-marketing in the 1990s. However, today, there is one critical and significant difference from these activities of the past in that the retailer is going to play a much greater role in how programming is developed and delivered. Today, manufacturers are playing on the retailer's field.

Over the past five years, retailers have come to understand that it is critically important that they build a differentiated image – one they need to guard jealously and protect at all cost. They have hired top-tier marketing personnel and learned that more than price alone gains shopper loyalty. They are no longer expecting to survive on manufacturer street money, and understand the importance of building the power of their brand and delivering solutions to their shoppers.

The result of this is that, sadly, retailers and brand marketers are suffering from a disconnect about the very meaning of the term 'shopper marketing'. Yes, they agree that it's about in-store and the 'first moment of truth'. Unfortunately, many manufacturers have yet to realize that it's the retailer – not the brand marketer – who is in control and dictating the terms.

Too many brand marketers are making the mistake of adopting the definition of shopper marketing offered by Deloitte & Touche: 'All marketing stimuli developed based on a deep understanding of shopper behaviour designed to build brand equity, engage the shopper and lead him/her to purchase.' This is a flawed definition because it disregards the retailer as the key decision maker. It also ignores the retailer's most critical objective, which is to provide shopper solutions and drive sales by category, not by brand. Retailers aren't thinking about CPG brand equity; they care only about their shoppers and providing them with solutions: in health care, pet care, household, meals, entertainment – you name it.

The reality is that shopper marketing, done correctly, isn't even about marketing in the conventional sense. Traditionally, marketing is mainly about communicating messages to consumers – mostly advertising of one kind or another. For retail, the goal is not just to communicate to – it is to offer solutions for – shoppers. That's what helps shoppers have a more satisfying shopping experience. So the objective of shopper marketing really is not about traditional marketing at all. It is about delivering shopper solutions. And that's a very different objective. Manufacturers need to stop treating shoppers as if they are consumers in search of brands. They are not. They are shoppers in search of solutions. Marketers need to plan accordingly.

Retailers certainly understand this, most notably Wal-Mart. Anyone who has spoken with the merchandising and marketing team at Wal-Mart lately knows that their directive to brands is to offer shoppers category solutions. Wal-Mart wants its suppliers to get together with each other as partners and come back with new and innovative ways to provide shoppers with better solutions. This is a radical shift.

In case its intentions are not clear, Wal-Mart has also issued a style guide that mandates displays to conform to the Wal-Mart look and feel. If you come to them with a display idea that is not done up in Wal-Mart 'blue', you might just have to take it straight to the back and toss it in their recycling bin.

This should come as no shock to anyone who has been following the power shift to retailers – from Wal-Mart on down – over the past decade or more. Retailers have been chasing a 'solutions' approach for quite some time now, utilizing their real estate to build their brands. They've also become far more demanding when it comes to the kinds of merchandising they will accept.

The difference is that the days of thinking of national brands in isolation at retail are ending – and, in fact, we might as well assume those days are over. If Wal-Mart is now saying that it wants brands to collaborate to create solutions – which it will present in Wal-Mart branded displays – then you can be sure that the rest of the retail industry is not far behind.

Engineering solutions

Working on shopper marketing programming with Wal-Mart, or any other retailer, means viewing manufacturer brands from their perspective. Ultimately, that means viewing brands in the context of what retailers are trying to communicate as their point of difference, and what that means is from their shoppers' perspective. The implications of this are huge.

It means manufacturers have to start thinking about brands as a solution and, as such, how they relate to brands made by other manufacturers. They need to dig in and really understand how shoppers view brands in combination with related products – how they might combine and re-combine to come up with a total solution.

For example, think about 'family fun' as a concept in search of a solution. A 'family fun' solution might include DVDs, video games, snacks and soft drinks. Think about how many different ways the concept of 'family fun' might manifest itself, find partners that want to work together to provide an innovative solution, and then bring that idea to the retailer.

If you're thinking about coughs and colds, then maybe you've got a hand sanitizer and tissues and a cough medicine bundled nicely in a single display. That would be a real service to shoppers, who rarely keep a stash of cold-care items in the bathroom. Usually, when we're sick we go out and buy them and are in no mood to navigate the entire store to find all the products we need.

In some cases, the retailer will orchestrate this type of total-solution delivery. But, if Wal-Mart is setting the standard, we can expect that they and other retailers will want us to come to them with ideas. The idea of brands working together in this way will have its complications, but such complications obviously pale by comparison to the prospect of losing the exposure opportunity at Wal-Mart or anywhere else.

A potentially more dangerous outcome would be for retailers to relegate national brands to a support proposition for their programming, which could highlight private-label offerings, or to dictate that manufacturers support their own pre-packaged programming and not allow anything apart from this in their stores.

In this new world, it is possible that some brands may be able to provide solutions on their own. But by and large it is a brand new day and one that calls for collaboration not only with retailers but also with other brands.

Adjacencies, insights and investments

Understanding adjacencies at retail is a major part of this trend because adjacencies can drive solutions. Sometimes a very simple but insightful placement can yield a remarkable result. For example, putting a display of antibacterial soap in the pet-food aisle might be an interesting idea. Many people associate pet care with dirty hands, and reminding them about that when and where they are thinking about their pets is a good shopper solution.

This points directly at another imperative – manufacturers need to invest more heavily in research that provides the kind of shopper insights required to arrive at the most complete and compelling solutions.

It is absolutely essential that they invest in tools that can tell them who lives in each store's trading area and what their problems might be so that they can offer relevant solutions and build merchandising plans accordingly. Is there a high incidence of heart issues? Diabetes?

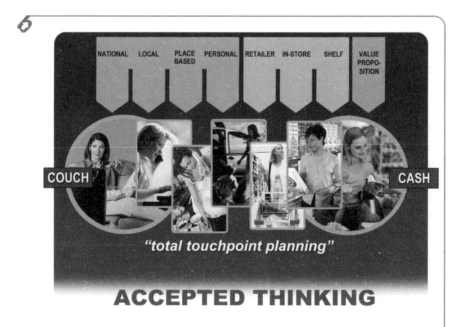

Figure 11.1 Total touchpoint planning

Seniors? Families with young children? Pets? They will need to know so they can provide relevant solutions.

This approach is also important in avoiding wasting resources. Suppose a new brand is planning a national introduction, with the same materials in every store. In a best-case scenario, this effort might get 70 per cent compliance – meaning that this brand would be wasting hundreds of thousands of marketing dollars (not to mention the environmental impact).

Speaking with shoppers

But, if they had done their homework and targeted just the right stores with just the right solutions, they would have had a very compelling retail story, driven growth and saved substantial funds. And, by the way, that homework also includes studying how to communicate effectively to shoppers. The most common mistake is simply transferring the creative from television commercials to in-store media.

While it's obviously important to keep a brand's identity consistent, it's equally important to keep it coherent. Too often, in-store communication assumes that the shopper remembers the brand's advertising. Even if recall is at a healthy level today – say, 25 per cent – that means 75 per cent of shoppers might have no idea what the slogan or tagline means.

A brand marketer would no more consider putting an ad on television without research to prove it works than jump out of the Empire State Building. And yet many marketers will spend a lot more money developing a shopper-marketing programme than they do on their television ads and place it in store without testing it. This is just wrong and has to change.

Shopper marketing is not about individual brands – it's not even about marketing in the usual sense. It's about communicating in a way that shoppers understand and appreciate, because it helps them find a solution to their needs and get the most out of their shopping trip.

The good news is that, in an increasingly complex marketing communications environment, the result is increased category sales, increased basket load – and growth for brands.

Part 2

Strategy: how to approach shopper marketing

12 Connecting, engaging and exciting shoppers

Michael Morrison and Meg Mundell

Michael Morrison is the programme director of the Monash Australian Marketing Study programme and coordinator of the Master of Marketing (Retailing) department of Monash University, Melbourne, Australia. Meg Mundell is a Melbourne-based writer, teacher and interdisciplinary researcher. Her journalism, creative writing and commentary have been widely published in Australian newspapers and journals.

Introduction

Shoppers are 'tuning out' when faced with traditional modes of in-store marketing. Their declining receptiveness poses a major dilemma for brands: how can they best build strong, lasting customer relationships?

Today's top brands are meeting the challenge by taking a personal approach: they set out to forge an emotional in-store connection with shoppers. Experiential shopper marketing (or emotional branding) signals a shift from simply selling products to selling experiences. This new and burgeoning field harnesses the power of the five senses to connect, engage and excite shoppers. The five case studies below offer a multi-sensory snapshot.

The eyes have it

Sight is humankind's most dominant sense, and this supremacy is underpinned in part by a profound connection to colour. Crayola's vibrant flagship store in Kansas City uses the emotional impact of colour to powerful effect. Within the store's bright, open-plan interior, colour not only imbues the space with a sense of energy and fun; it also operates as an orientating device, product identifier and invitation to play. Children can interact with a wall-size 'colour mosaic', play a colour-coded game of noughts and crosses, spin a colour wheel, or take a brightly coloured seat at a mini-sized communal table to create vivid drawings. The store's layout encourages young brand users to connect and engage – not only with the brand's products, but also with parents, siblings, staff and each other.

Figure 12.1 Crayola's flagship store in Kansas City

This Crayola store also has a branded on-site café, a communal space where families can come together to relax, refuel and re-energize before heading home with their purchases – or perhaps taking the opportunity to revisit the retail area. Once again, the café is a vibrant, open space that uses colour to stimulate the senses, reinforce the brand image, and link with specific products. Its airy interior features circle shapes and rippling lines of colour, calling to mind the brand's signature crayon products.

A solid banner curving overhead lists the energetic names of specific hues, including 'hot magenta', 'outrageous orange' and 'unmellow yellow', while a decorative central display employs cylinders of bright fruit to create a visual link between colour and food.

A harmonious relationship

Sound is a crucial component of atmosphere, and its most powerful manifestation can be found in music. In an in-store context, this principle is applied effectively by Abercrombie & Fitch, which positions itself as a fashion-oriented casual-apparel brand aimed at young 'aspirational' consumers (aged 15–28) desiring 'an American college lifestyle'. A&F carefully tailors its in-store music to match the tastes and preferences of its target market, using a customized playlist to create an interior soundscape in close harmony with the brand's own image – upbeat, energetic, fun, youthful, carefree and high-volume. In an auditory sense, the in-store atmosphere is reminiscent of a nightclub or dance party.

Figure 12.2 In-store environment, Abercrombie & Fitch

The strategic use of this highly charged music not only attracts passing shoppers into the A&F store; it also functions as a potent brand connection, engagement and excitement mechanism. Recent studies on the relationship between in-store music and brand positioning have underlined the connecting, engaging and exciting power of this aural medium. A&F's in-store music is an excellent example of brand strategy 'fit' – that is, the harmonious alignment of shoppers' first-hand perceptions with their prior expectations of the brand.

The impact of perceived music 'fit' and 'misfit' was the focus of a study in 2006. In-depth interviews with shoppers found that a perceived music–brand 'misfit' – a poor match between the music played and the brand's perceived image – could lead to a decline in consumer–brand relationships. Conversely, a synergistic fit could enhance and reinforce that relationship.

Scents of place

One of our most powerful yet often overlooked senses, smell, taps directly into the emotions, memory and subconscious mind. A growing number of retailers are capitalizing on the subliminal impact of aroma by using in-store (or ambient) fragrancing to enhance brand image and influence shopper behaviour.

Supré, an Australian-based fashion chain targeted towards 14- to 28-year-old females, is one example. The brand took part in a 2007 study to investigate how in-store atmospherics – specifically, the combined use of pleasant fragrance and loud, club-style music – impacted on shopping behaviour and satisfaction levels. The study examined shoppers' approach, behaviour, time spent in-store, money spent in-store and evaluation of overall satisfaction.

Figure 12.3 Supré, an Australian-based fashion chain

Emotions are known to play a major role in the way consumers behave while shopping. A pleasant but subtle vanilla aroma, particularly when paired with loud music, was found to exert a positive influence on the emotional state of shoppers, enhancing both the retail ambience and the shopping experience.

The findings of the study provided specific knowledge of how sensory aspects of the retail environment influence shoppers' emotional states. In particular, when developing in-store shopping environments, retailers should consider music volume and aroma as instruments for creating more positive moods and behaviours. Careful tailoring of these variables can translate to unique store atmospherics, a point of differentiation and a significant competitive advantage.

The power of touch

Apple's flagship stores in New York, Chicago, London and Tokyo are designed to encourage shoppers' physical, tactile and personal engagement. The smooth, clean lines of these spaces echo both the brand's stylish and functional image and the distinctive design of its products. Ample seating encourages visitors to linger and mingle, rounded edges and curved handrails invite touch, and glass staircases and walls transmit a sense of spaciousness, clarity and light.

At Apple's stores, touch also takes on a personalized, 'hands-on' dimension: visitors are encouraged to use the products on-site, a strategy that promotes direct tactile interaction with the brand, and young users have their own custom-sized communal space. Shoppers can also learn about all Apple's products at an in-store theatre, take part in knowledge transfer activities by testing new software in the 'studio', or converse face to face with 'Apple geniuses', expert helpers situated at the in-store 'genius bar'.

This latter example shows how Apple engages the power of 'personal touch', extending the brand's philosophy into the social realm. The people who staff Apple stores form an integral part of the overall shopping experience. Apple employees don't look like usual retail staff: instead of name tags, they have business cards, and of course they all carry iPods and iPhones on their belts. They don't merely work for the brand – they live the lifestyle experiences that Apple is selling to customers.

Taste sensation

Taste is a key element of the Dean & Deluca store, an upmarket food provider in SoHo, New York. The brand states its mission as being the 'exploration, discovery, and celebration of food from around the globe', and the store showcases a vast array of beautifully merchandised premium produce. The senses are stimulated via attractive presentation, an atmosphere of abundance and variety, and a 'retail theatre'. Visitors encounter a series of enticing micro-environments, each with a particular ambience and emotional resonance. Numerous tasting samples engage them directly in the food experience and encourage them to purchase.

Figure 12.4 Dean & Deluca store, SoHo, New York

Food carries long-held associations of community – connotations of breaking bread, sharing a meal and meeting up for a great cup of coffee. Dean & Deluca's culinary associations have deliberately been given a social dimension with the inclusion of an in-store café. The store is one of New York's most popular meeting places, which in turn fosters shoppers' sense of personal connection and engagement with the brand's place, space and experience. In a deliberate move towards the 'village economy', the store presents itself as a community site, a meaningful and interconnected social sphere, rather than merely a space where goods are sold.

The brand's identification with 'taste' extends to the sense of personal preference. The store's interior suggests indulgence and luxury, and offers fresh flowers, books, homewares, gifts and a range of other appealing products. Staff recruitment, selection and reward practices are likewise designed to reinforce the brand's culture.

My place, my space, my experience

These examples of successful shopper marketing strategies highlight a definite shift towards a new shopping paradigm, one that is increasingly personalized, connected, active and experience based. Through engaging the five senses, emotional branding connects with shoppers on this more immediate level. It should be noted that, while customizing in-store atmospherics does require 'zooming in' on each specific sense, the best results stem from a holistic approach that engages all five senses: sight, sound, smell, touch and taste.

As in-store environments continue to evolve, this will create opportunities for even deeper levels of connection, engagement and excitement. Tomorrow's shoppers will play a more active role in personalizing their own shopping encounters. They will become, in effect, 'co-creators' of retail atmospheres: joint authors of a customized place, space and experience based on their own needs, desires, preferences and emotions.

13 Tailing your shoppers: retailing for the future

AnnaMaria M Turano

AnnaMaria M Turano is an executive director of MCAworks. She leads client engagements involving corporate and product brand strategy, customer value proposition development and new product development. She is the co-author of *Stopwatch Marketing*. MCAworks is a management consulting firm based in Westport, CT, USA, which is dedicated to helping clients accelerate and sustain business growth via action-oriented sales and marketing strategies.

Retailing versus routine

Imagine that shopping was no longer seen as an obligatory activity checked off on customers' daily or weekend 'to do' list. Imagine that shopping was an anticipated everyday part of customers' daily routine – just like going for a run before work or meeting friends after work. It should be the key objective of any retailer to make shopping a natural experience – seamlessly woven into how and where customers now live and work.

E-tailing: reaching customers at home and at work

The proliferation of online shopping was critical in driving retailers to understand that shopping does not need to be confined to their physical storefronts; customers appreciate the ease, convenience and privacy of being able to shop online. Many retailers found new customers as a result – new customers who might never visit the store in person owing to time or geographical constraints.

Small boutiques as well as large chains benefited from making their online presence known and readily accessible. A small skincare line (such as Santa Maria Novella in Florence) could now attract customers from all corners of the globe who appreciate the centuries-old formula and distinctive packaging. A large apparel chain (such as Bloomingdale's in New York) could now reach those customers who didn't live near an outlet but had always dreamed of shopping at the fabled institution. And web-only retailers (such as Zappos, which started off as an online shoe salon) emerged as competitive retailers, despite never having established an actual storefront.

Customers were happy to shop 24/7 from home, work or school, and on their computer as well as their mobile phone. Information (price, quality, availability, fit) became readily available, and satisfied as well as dissatisfied customers became all too eager to share their musings and recommendations with other shoppers.

However, e-tailing is just a small stepping stone to the future of retailing. Customers will still balance shopping in-store versus

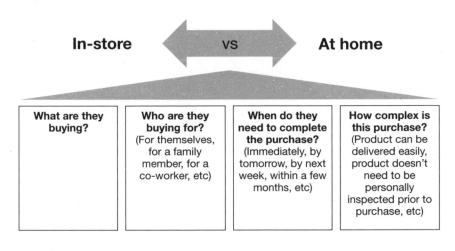

Figure 13.1 In-store vs at home

shopping at home, depending on what and when they are buying. Just extending a store's products and service on to the web overlooks the drivers behind the growth in online shopping.

Tailing: innovating retail for the future

Any successful retail strategy is built around the target customers' needs and wants – it all starts and ends with the target's behaviour. Customers want to dictate how, when and where they shop – and retailers today must listen and redesign their retail concepts around customers' lifestyles in order to be successful tomorrow.

The future of retailing lies in the idea of 'tailing' – following the target customers' behaviour patterns and designing retail concepts to mesh better with customers' daily activities such as commuting, chauffeuring their family, managing their household and running errands. 'Tailing' takes the practice of retail to where and how customers live and work. As a result, the activity of shopping is seen as less disruptive and more routine to everyday life.

Innovative retailers are beginning to move closer to their customers in order to better tailor their products, services and retail concepts to the targets' wants and needs.

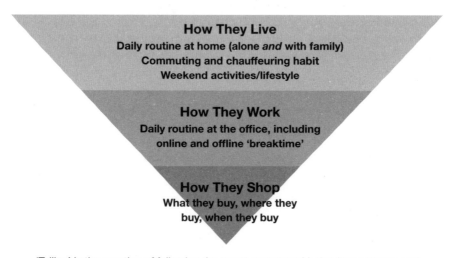

'Tailing' is the practice of following the target customers' behaviour patterns and designing retail concepts to mesh better with customers' lifestyles. Tailing takes the practice of retail to *where and how* customers live and work.

Figure 13.2 Tailing pyramid

Tailing in Roppongi Hills: comfort and convenience

Roppongi Hills bills itself as an 'artelligent city' – a city within a city (Tokyo) built to meet the weekday and weekend needs of its resident population. The multi-block 'city' is an exciting, upscale offering of residences, retailers, restaurants and cultural venues designed to integrate seamlessly in how Roppongi residents live, work, shop, eat and relax.

Unlike its counterpart Omotesando Hills (also a Mori-designed complex), Roppongi Hills uniquely succeeds because it foremost serves the needs of its target, with variety in residences (high-rise and low-rise apartments), shops (clothing and home furnishings for business, sport, special events and children) and restaurants (Japanese, Italian, Chinese, French, steakhouses, coffee bars, ice cream parlours, to name a few), as well as being an attractive destination for the rest of Tokyo. Conveniently located near the Roppongi metro stop, residents must walk through the complex on their way home. The 'forced commute' leads residents through the various buildings and open public spaces. The architectural design (eg the form, colours, materials, layout and ambience) of the buildings and spaces effectively balance high-tech, modern materials with a soothing organic tone. The result serves to help residents and visitors switch from the busy workday into evening leisure time. In effect, the daily commute becomes a daily stroll as residents slow down to chat with fellow neighbours and absorb the retail offerings on their way home.

Roppongi Hills' success is driven by an appreciation of its residents' time constraints in the evenings and at weekends. By effectively integrating retail (as well as restaurant and cultural offerings) into how and where customers ultimately live, Roppongi Hills created a neighbourhood bubble that its residents appreciate and reward with their time and money.

Tailing in Nau: webfront meets the homefront

Designed around a 'business unusual' model that integrates economic, environment and social factors, Nau is a lifestyle outdoor sports apparel brand that sought to reinvent the way people shop by 'tailing' their storefronts and websites to the passions of environmentally minded people.

A focus on the environment pervaded Nau's retail strategy. In an effort to reduce unnecessary space and minimize store rents, Nau's stores had much smaller footprints compared to similar boutiques. The in-store materials were predominantly recyclable – very much in line with their target customers' green lifestyle. These storefronts were actually webfronts where customers browse through a handful of styles and sizes, try on samples in the fitting rooms, and make their purchases via a self-serve kiosk. And, in keeping with the environmental focus, Nau's customers were incentivized with a 10 per cent discount to ship their purchases home rather than carrying them right out of the store.

The webfront approach was built on understanding how Nau's target customers live and work. By giving their customers 'less' – for example, one size in each sample to try on (the ultimate colour choice is made at the self-serve kiosk) and no bag to carry out of the store entrance, Nau was able to give the community 'more' – more money donated to environmental and social causes chosen by the customer.

Nau's goals were to create a passionate, engaged community – not merely a brand. Just as customers were driven to the self-serve kiosks to make purchases, customers were also driven to the web to learn more and contribute to the communal heart of Nau. Its website was full of stories – stories from customers as well as employees (from management to interns) discussing their active outdoor pursuits as well as their daily attempts to live closer to the Earth, whether driving hybrid cars or riding bikes to work or increasingly eating or using natural and organic household products. The sharing of these day-in-the-life stories and weekend experiences united customers and employees alike into a higher-minded community – not just a group of Nau fans.

Alas, Nau's original retail concept might have been ahead of its time. Despite overwhelming media praise and an ambitious expansion strategy in its first year, Nau closed down retail operations after only 15 months and five storefronts in the United States owing to the credit crunch. Nevertheless, the Nau brand lives on – selling online direct to customers as well as via other established retailers.

The lesson learned from Nau is that retailing today is a hybrid of offline and online behaviours. More and more customers are accumulating information and trial in-store before purchasing online in order to optimize price, convenience and timing – or vice versa. Retailers that embrace and promote this hybrid shopping activity will ultimately distinguish themselves as being attuned to how customers want to live and shop.

Tailing in Boots: location is everything

Boots is the United Kingdom's leading pharmacy-led health and beauty retailer, with over 2,600 locations. The chances are that the average Londoner walks by two to three Boots locations in the daily commute to and from the office. These locations are not left to chance. Boots knows the chain needs to be in the locations their customers want – in order to be the retailer of choice for any quick errand or emergency need.

Boots' success derives from their objective to be omnipresent in their customers' lives. Store rents may be cheaper at more out-of-the-way locations but foot traffic would surely be less. And customer reliance on Boots' uncanny knack to have exactly what they need, regardless of location, would surely drop off. In effect, Boots practically shows up at the customer's doorstep whenever and wherever the need arises.

By understanding that its busy, often-harried customer wants to get in and out of the store quickly, Boots capitalizes on its strength in product assortment, friendly service, fast queues and strategically placed locations.

Summary

Retail success will be based on how well you know and act upon how your customers behave. Understanding how they shop is not enough to be competitive; retailers must understand how their customers live and evolve their retail concepts accordingly.

Lifestyle marketing is at the heart of future retail success. By 'tailing' customers and following their daily life and work behaviour patterns, retailers can identify the pain points of shopping (eg out-of-the-way locations, noisy stores, confusing layouts, long checkout queues) and redesign the overall shopping experience to better integrate with how customers actually live and want to live. Work and household management is hard enough; shopping shouldn't have to be.

14 Retail media: a catalyst for shopper marketing

Gwen Morrison

Gwen Morrison is the CEO, the Americas and Australasia of The Store, WPP's global retail practice, which brings together the collective retail knowledge and skill sets of one of the world's largest marketing services groups.

Over the past few years, in-store media technology has become better, cheaper and more compelling. The placement and content of the configurations of retail networks continue to improve. In conjunction with an increasingly fragmented media landscape, this improvement and proliferation of technology ought to prompt a fundamental reconsideration of the relationship between brands and their in-store captive audiences.

However, the majority of in-store networks have struggled to meet their targets and deliver real value for the shopper. In the rush to install these networks, insufficient thought has been given to marketing intent and to the planned operationalizing of that intent. The placement of screens has often been an afterthought, with monitors that shoppers must strain to view. Content has been out of sync with product placement and shopper needs. A 30-minute cooking show pulled from a cable TV network offers a hurried shopper little value. Most importantly, the 'dynamic' aspect of in-store media has been woefully underutilized. Originally, the fundamental purpose of in-store media was to have point-of-purchase communication that could be programmed to match specific and variable shopper needs and behaviours. But when playlogs are repeated for two-week flights, there cannot be an alignment between shopper insights and retail communications. The scepticism about the real value of in-store networks may reflect the failure to conceptualize and employ these resources properly, rather than represent an accurate assessment of their considerable potential.

However, while the networks have not lived up to expectations, the focus of store-as-active-medium has had the collateral benefit of helping companies rethink their strategic conception of communicating with shoppers. Rather than a broad-based communication through traditional media, in-store media offered the possibility of a direct message to a nearly ideal targeted audience, with a corresponding decrease in media cost per target viewer. Early champions of in-store TV brought significant attention to the value of communicating with the shopper at closest proximity to purchase. Why wouldn't an advertiser try to reach the shopper at the critical moment of decision? The industry benchmarks, initially commissioned by POPAI, claimed that high percentages of purchase decisions were made in-store. This armed the media owners with convincing data that drew more attention to the store. We have seen customer marketing teams arm themselves with 'point of decision' insights to advocate their brand programmes to leading retailers. Much of this has been fuelled by the retail media industry.

I would suggest that, with all their faults, in-store media developments closely correlate with the advancement of shopper marketing. When Wal-Mart TV in the United States was first promoted as the fifth largest media network buy in the country, new statistics about shopper behaviour and the notion of marketing directly to the shopper came into play. A number of FMCG marketing departments started to look

Figure 14.1 The Walmart Smart Network generates information on shopper response by product and daypart

at in-store communications strategically as 'unpurchased media'. They also started to recognize that the rich investments in their brand advertising were not correlating with retail POP. Major brands began assessing the media value of in-store communications and investing more in their development, particularly in the area of shopper insights.

In-store media have also fuelled the promotion industry's opportunity to rise in the marketing mix. As modalities for in-store advertising were established, promotion agencies began to advocate that 'below the line' services must be seen in a strategic brand framework. They began to develop metrics to quantify this opportunity. For example, the number of seconds a shopper looked at a display was now a return on media investment. In-store 'GRPs' were calculated for each key retailer.

Another significant outcome of in-store media developments is an improved understanding of how to engage shoppers from the perspectives of the creative-generated content and design. We know shoppers are not in the same mood or mode as consumers at home, and the same shopper varies in his or her needs and behaviours during different trips. The initial shortcomings of creative content delivered in retail networks underscored the dos and don'ts when it comes to connecting with shoppers.

Here are a few basic principles:

- *Put the right message in the right place.* The ultimate benefit of in-store communications is that we are able to target shoppers in specific departments, at the point of decision. During the development and sell-in stage, most media owners have promoted this. But we continue to see ads for products that are not within view of the screen. Personal care products may run in the produce department and promotional offers for grocery items in the checkout lane, long after shoppers have passed the corresponding displays. Through misalignment in placement, brands miss their opportunity to connect with shoppers when they are actively engaged in the category. The more we mismatch content with locale, the more the shopper rejects the medium. Bringing the message closer to the product, perhaps coupled with logical adjacencies, allows the shopper to respond to the message. These learnings, obvious as they seem, are beginning to drive the technology developments as well. Smaller screens that are integrated into the shelf (rather than large overhead monitors) are becoming the standard.
- *Deliver the right message at the right time.* We know that the pace and mission of the shopper are different throughout the week at a typical grocery, mass-market or hypermarket store. For example,

price-sensitive seniors may be shopping on a Tuesday morning, while the 4 to 6 pm dinner rush is made up of hurried shoppers, more focused on meals and convenience. One of the great advantages of in-store media is flexibility. It offers the opportunity to customize promotional offers to the types of shoppers in the store at any given time. Yet, as this book goes to press, we don't see the majority of retail media networks (or their advertisers) developing playlogs that match shopper insights with real-time messaging. What we do see is deeper analytics that drive more successful approaches to merchandising, but they are in an early stage of adoption. Wal-Mart's Smart Network in the US may be leading the industry with enhanced analytics. Ultimately, with new tools that match in-store advertising with register data, the dynamic opportunity of digital media will be realized.

- *Inspire the shopper.* As the industry begins to pinpoint time and place for effective content, it is important to recognize the context. Some product categories are more conducive to information-based messages, while others can support broader inspirational imagery and content. A few retailers such as Target in the United States have carefully considered this issue. Target's content for Channel Red merges the retailer's appealing brand imagery with carefully developed vendor brand content. This approach has been shown to increase dwell time and purchases in the electronics category. Translating these learnings to other areas of the store is the opportunity to be tapped. As shoppers wait in line at a pharmacy, there is ample opportunity to inspire them with broader ideas about health, wellness and lifestyle that can result in significant incremental purchases.

Media Targets the Shopper

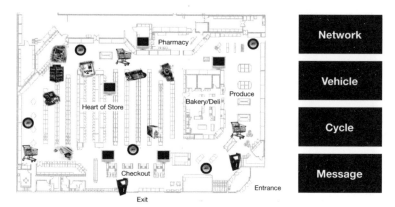

Figure 14.2 Media target the shopper

The consolidation of retail and the emergence of in-store media are contributing to a new shopper-centric landscape. Bryan Gildenberg of MVI framed this nicely when he talked about branding within an environment of choice. In advertising, we traditionally build affinity and demand for brands. At retail we have to persuade shoppers to buy when they are faced with a myriad of choice. So, while the retail media shareholders have promoted this opportunity with vigour, the real momentum has been within FMCG organizations that are putting shopper marketing into practice. Richer understanding of the potential of all retail touchpoints is driving a more complex brand framework, from home to shelf to register.

The new shopper-centric landscape and new metrics will help put shopper-facing communications on a level playing field with other media. As our ability to speak to the shopper with measured results develops, our approach to building brands may shift dramatically.

15 Integrated communications planning for shopper marketing

David Sommer

David Sommer is managing partner of MEC Retail for Mediaedge:cia (MEC). MEC Retail offers a consultancy for manufacturers and retailers in using in-store communication both strategically and creatively. MEC gets consumers actively engaged with our clients' brands, leading to positive awareness, deeper relationships and stronger sales.

Integrated Communications Planning

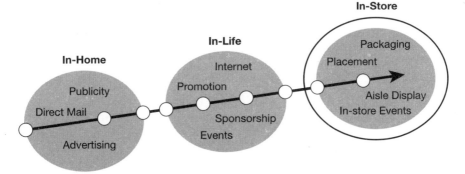

Figure 15.1 Integrated communications planning

The 'target consumer' – moving out of the cross-hairs

Advertising executives used to talk obsessively about 'reaching' consumers. 'Who is our target? How do we reach them as efficiently and effectively as possible with a differentiated and relevant message about our product?' In the old days, the simplest of business equations told the whole story: revenue minus cost equals profit. Revenue was driven by more 'consumer targets' becoming buyers. Then we subtracted how much the customer acquisition effort cost and simply computed our profits. We adjusted the marketing mix annually, and the cycle of assault on 'consumer targets' continued.

Technology has created a world where consumers no longer have targets painted on their foreheads, and the usual marketing weapons miss the mark. Consumers control the who, what, when and where of 'being reached'. Now, consumers actually 'reach out' and 'opt in' for the marketing experiences they choose. The demise of the 'target consumer' has led to the 'controlling consumer'.

Evolution of media and retail – engaging consumers who are in control

Don't get me wrong; at-home media such as network television still matter. Vast numbers of consumers opt in to watch *Grey's Anatomy* and *American Idol* during prime time, but, make no mistake about it, consumers who sit on their couch and watch their network TV 'real-time', commercials and all, are choosing to do so. They are opting in for the old-fashioned watch-it-with-the-rest-of-the-world, water-cooler experience. These consumers had a choice of watching time-shifted TV on their TIVO, downloading to their iPods or streaming the video in their offices the next day over high-speed connections.

If you are vigorously nodding your head 'yes' or, more likely, thinking 'Tell me something I do not already know', just wait. We are going to segue into the subject at hand, marketing at retail.

What does all of this talk about 'consumers opting in' for content have to do with retail? Theoretically, consumers opt in to physically visiting a retail store in much the same way as they tune into ABC for an episode of *Grey's Anatomy*. However, something happens when consumers embark on a trip to the store – they change from consumers to shoppers. Consumers get into their car to achieve some specific goal:

The 'store' has become increasingly more important as a way to reach our consumers...

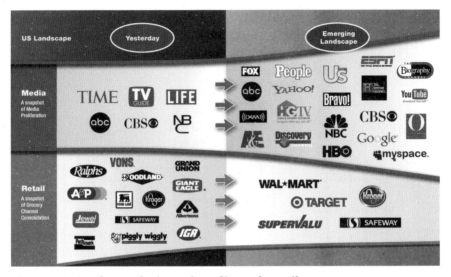

Figure 15.2 The evolution of media and retail

stock up on groceries, buy a flat screen LCD TV or buy some new work clothes. Each one of these very different 'trips' places the shopper in a completely different mode and mindset.

For example, when a mother is rushing to stock up for a family of four young children, she wants to spend as little time and money as possible, find healthy foods, grab a cup of coffee for herself as a pick-me-up and maybe enjoy the simple pleasure of a weekly magazine while standing in the checkout line. When she goes shopping for the stock-up grocery trip she is not opting in for a 30-second TV spot on a video screen hanging from the ceiling. For marketing materials to have a chance of engaging her in-store, they need to add real value to her life. In this hypothetical example, a screen running a clever 30-second TV spot for Danimals (a children's yogurt drink) might not get noticed. It might not be relevant to the shopper's planned trip or need state. However, a little detective work might uncover a 'shopper insight' that the parent would really like all of the healthy dairy products for children placed in one special section of the refrigerated aisle and not necessarily with the other yogurts.

Creating a 'healthy children dairy section' might not sound like a brilliant marketing vehicle for Danimals. However, in the context of our earlier discussion about consumers being in control and 'opting in' for the marketing experiences they choose, a shopping time-saver programme for a busy parent could create a relevant touchpoint.

Collaborative marketing

Figure 15.3 Collaborative marketing

By listening to shoppers and understanding what types of experiences they will opt in for we can craft a winning marketing at retail plan. In the end, it boils down to that magical 'vin' diagram where consumers are on top and marketers and retailers work together to create the optimal shopper experience and the elusive win–win–win.

Measuring the effectiveness of the store as a marketing weapon

If we picture that fictitious 'healthy children dairy section' we just imagined where parents can breeze by, browse the healthiest of dairy products, examine nutritional information and fill their cart with a variety of old favourites and some guaranteed healthy new products, how would we measure this in-store activity? What is the value of Danimals being highlighted and giving attention-grabbing signage in this special section?

The answers to these questions require a closer look at our definition of in-store media. If we ripped the roof off an individual store and looked inside for an aerial view at all the places we can engage consumers, all of these options qualify as in-store media.

Our definition of retail media also includes all of the places where marketers can use retail as a channel to engage consumers. Think

Figure 15.4 In-store media

direct mail pieces sent out by the retailers to a targeted list. Think frequent shopper card programmes. Imagine a situation where Best Buy knows I am in the market for an LCD flat screen TV based on my prior purchases and the information I have provided at their website. Panasonic can then work with Best Buy to mail me a brochure from Best Buy and Panasonic that I will opt in to read, cover to cover, even though I know these are just marketing materials.

Just to reiterate, our definition of marketing at retail includes all of the ways marketers can engage consumers using retailers (their stores, their mailing lists, their relationships) as a communications channel. With this in mind, we must carefully evaluate and measure all of the value we as marketers gain from each engagement of shoppers through the retail channel.

There are three major buckets of measurement: media value, brand metrics and sales lift. Media value considers things like: store traffic multiplied by aisle traffic multiplied by compliance equals in-store media value. Brand metrics is more like traditional advertising measures, which include tracking studies to determine brand health as a result of advertising communications. In the case on in-store communications, intercepts are often the easiest way to understand how a 'control' and 'exposed' group feel about a brand. The final bucket is sales lift: if our baseline volume was 'X', the incremental volume is 'X'+?.

Measurement = 3 big buckets

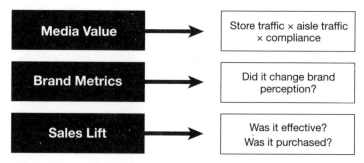

Figure 15.5 Three big buckets

Most marketers and sociologists agree that this 'controlling consumer' is here to stay. And most marketers also agree that consumers will continue to embark on shopping trips where they transform into shoppers. Given these strong convictions, we must examine the barriers that have hindered the development of shopper insights and ultimately shopper marketing.

Seven barriers to development of shopper marketing

1. Organizational structure and budget allocations based on old priorities.
2. Not many leading marketing executives who are also qualified shopper marketers.
3. Lack of real shopper insights and shopper research.
4. Legacy processes and the challenges of current advertising process timing.
5. No current standards of measurement for in-store activity.
6. Using retail as media is not easy, not turn-key like buying media. Finding the win–win–win for consumers, retailers and marketers is very difficult.
7. Retailers are not really media moguls. Their first priority is to sell more product, to more people, more often *not* to monetize their stores as true media.

Right place, wrong time

As Dr John (famous New Orleans jazz and funk singer) once said, 'I been in the right place, but it must have been the wrong time.' There is no question marketing at retail is the 'right place'. Consumers continue to opt in for the most interactive of experiences, shopping. And, with 138 million consumers walking through a Wal-Mart every week, consumers are doing so in large numbers. However, for much of my career, I believe it was the wrong time for shopper marketers. Given the mass reach, prominence and glamour of traditional advertising, marketing at retail was relegated to a secondary service function within marketing organizations.

Things have changed. Almost every day I hear about marketing executives who are reshaping their organizations to create a tighter focus on this key area. Sometimes they call it shopper marketing, FMOT (first moment of truth marketing), red zone, category management or collaborative marketing, but we just call it marketing at retail. And, for marketing executives committed to getting results and maximizing ROI, the potential for actively engaging shoppers at retail is enormous.

16 The conversion model for shopper research

Clemens Steckner

Clemens Steckner is a managing partner of the g/d/p Research Group. He runs the shopper research division, and develops innovative methods for POS research. G/d/p Research Group was founded in 1977 as an independent market research company whose speciality areas include shopper, category and retail research.

More than 10,000 products compete to catch the eye of shoppers in a typical supermarket. The customer selects 10 or 20 products to take home, but how does he or she make this choice? What are the factors that influence purchasing behaviour? And how does the colourful clamour of shopper marketing work?

Shopper research deals with the process of searching for a product, making a decision, and purchasing directly at the point of sale. Most purchase decisions are not made until the customer is in the shop. The jumble of products and marketing measures runs the risk of causing shopper confusion, with the result that no purchase is made. Optimizing the purchasing process, for instance by providing clearer orientation, makes for contented customers who are also more willing to part with their cash.

Shopper research considers the various aspects of the purchasing process. What do shoppers have in their trolley? How do they behave during a purchase? What are the motives behind the purchase? Only when the sales figures are viewed together with objectively identifiable purchasing behaviour and conscious and unconscious decision processes can a true insight be gained into the purchasing process. These insights can be used to improve POS strategies, ranging from the placement and presentation of goods to pricing and product design,

Figure 16.1 Shopper research

thereby ensuring a smooth purchase without distractions, high conversion rates and minimal loss of potential buyers.

The conversion model helps in recognizing optimization potential at the POS. The purchase process is broken down into individual conversion stages, from frequency and attention to information, comparison and purchase. For each of these conversion stages, both missed and achieved conversion potential need to be analysed.

First of all, let's take a bird's-eye view of the whole shop-floor area of a retail outlet. How do the shoppers move around the store, what

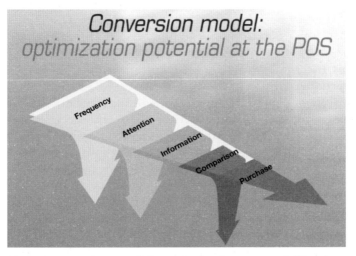

Figure 16.2 Conversion model: optimization potential in the purchasing process

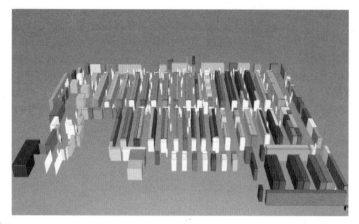

Figure 16.3 Customer path

are the main routes, where can they get information and how much is purchased at different times? These questions can be answered in detail using shopper path studies.

Shopper path studies reveal all activities at the POS as regards actions, movement and time in a real, natural purchasing situation. A particularly suitable method of doing this is a computer-assisted observation and recording of customer behaviour. The data provide different ways of analysing customer frequency, information search and product access. The result can show each shelf, each freezer and each display in terms of shopper frequency and purchase probability.

In the three-dimensional computer animation, every last corner of the store can be examined. The shelves are colour-coded to show customer frequency and the probability of purchase. The data are used as the basis for concrete recommendations for optimizing layout concepts, product range, product positioning, and promotions.

One of the key figures when deciding on the placement of the various product groups in the POS is frequency elasticity, that is, how the probability of purchase varies with shopper frequency. 'Inelastic' product groups, such as household products, should be placed where the frequency is low, but 'elastic' products such as confectionery should be placed in high-frequency areas. If shopper interest and purchase probability do not increase despite the higher frequency, the layout concept should be improved, as it appears that attention is not sufficiently attracted. The effect of POS tools such as in-store TV is also highly dependent on customer frequency. They can only achieve their full effect in heavily trafficked areas.

Now let's leave the bird's-eye view in order to home in on a single shelf. Observation procedures covering a high number of cases make it possible to carry out detailed analyses of the conversion stages at the shelf, right down to the level of individual products. For instance, the shopper research box records shopper behaviour in full detail through an automatic process. The box tracks all shopper movements and changes on the shelf, without compromising data privacy. The knowledge gained in this way concerning information and decision patterns at the shelf allows product placement to be optimized and full advantage to be taken of shelf adjacencies.

This has been shown time and again in studies carried out for consumer goods industries. Changing the shelf layout to make it easier to find the products means that a significantly higher proportion of those seeking information about a product end up making a purchase – and they spend less time deciding. It's also possible to show just how much signs or banners improve customer flow rates along the shelf.

Besides these conversion stages, access patterns are a great help when it comes to improving placement. As regards complex shelves, in particular, it is very important to support cross-buying patterns by placing products with a view to the target group. Shelves organized in this way fully exploit the shelf's purchase potential.

To really get to the bottom of the conversion process, while also establishing the link between customer frequency and information or purchase, we need to understand the shopper's perception of the POS. What do shoppers pay attention to? Do they even notice ceiling danglers, wobblers, signage and the like? The 'eye sensor' offers new possibilities of biotic attention measurement; it can tell if a human eye looks directly at it. The way a shopper naturally pays attention to different things can therefore be measured. For instance, this makes it possible to investigate the precise effect of adverts on in-store TV.

Together with the analysis of scanner data and surveys, these shopper observations make it possible to decode the purchasing process. The optimization of POS concepts using this knowledge is of benefit for retailers, manufacturers and customers. Stores can make the best possible use of every corner of the retail outlet, manufacturers benefit from the best possible visibility for their products, and simplified orientation means shoppers can find their way around the POS with fewer problems.

Surveys confirm that shoppers want better orientation in the POS. Forty-one per cent would find it easier to manage their grocery shopping if purchasing was simplified using more aids to guide them such as shelf signage. Almost 30 per cent see clearer organization of goods as the most important aspect (g/d/p Research Group data, March–June 2006).

If you have to spend a long time looking for something, you are likely to give up altogether. Fifty-three per cent of shoppers have sometimes ended up not buying a product because they didn't want to look for it any more. In hypermarkets, the figure is as high as 62 per cent. Thirty per cent also say they would be more inclined to buy more products if only they could find them more quickly (g/d/p Research Group data, March–June 2006).

The only way to make the best use of purchasing potential is to know how shoppers search for products and decide what to buy, and organize placement accordingly. This makes it less likely the shopper will change to a different product or abandon the purchase. Therefore it is even more important to make regular assessments and improvements. In view of increasingly shorter product life cycles and more innovative categories, purchasing behaviour is constantly changing. It is worth carrying out regular optimizations – shorter search times lead to greater customer satisfaction and a greater willingness to spend. Retailers and industry both benefit from this. And, not least, shoppers do too, because it makes shopping more fun.

Figure 16.4 Shopper confusion

17 In-store measurements for optimizing shopper marketing

Rajeev Sharma

Dr Rajeev Sharma is the founder and CEO of VideoMining Corporation. He is credited with pioneering research on automatic human behaviour analysis and human–computer interaction. VideoMining Corporation is focused on providing real-time shopper insights to retailers, consumer products manufacturers and media stakeholders.

With the increasing focus on the store as the place to win over consumers, there is a pressing need today to understand the shopping process in depth. This understanding is crucial for designing marketing and merchandising strategies that are relevant to the shoppers. When the consumers enter the store and become shoppers, their expectations change. Understanding and meeting those expectations is the key to winning the in-store battle for both retailers and manufacturers.

We need measurement tools that provide direct visibility into the shopper decision process and enable marketing metrics for improving every retail touchpoint. Major attempts have been made recently to fill this gap in shopper knowledge. The most visible effort has been the PRISM project pioneered by the In-Store Marketing Institute and syndicated by Nielsen In-Store. PRISM responds to the specific need to make the store comparable with traditional media by offering a rating system. It employs infrared sensors to get traffic counts at different parts of the store to measure the 'opportunity to see'.

While traffic measures can be used for rating the store as a marketing medium, traffic sensors do not offer visibility into shopper behaviour, especially in relation to specific store elements. This leaves a critical gap in the information capture for shopper marketing, failing to provide visibility into shopper engagement, shopper demographics and other relevant shopper metrics.

Traditional research methods such as video-based observation and survey methods are used in an ad hoc way today to meet the need for shopper insights. Such manual methods are subjective, expensive and under-sampled, and thus not scalable. There is an urgent need for automation in the process of gathering rich shopper data to have a scalable measurement solution for retail.

A breakthrough measurement platform using in-store video

A recent technology breakthrough has led to the development of an in-store measurement platform that fills the need for automatically capturing shopper data. The in-store video platform uses software to measure the behaviour and demographics (gender, age range and ethnicity) of shoppers, and can provide detailed data about entire shopping trips. The measurement technologies evolved from R&D, and span over a decade through projects with US government agencies such as the Department of Defense, the Department of Homeland Security and the National Science Foundation.

Software can now continuously 'watch' in-store video to provide a wealth of shopper behaviour and demographics data. The breakthrough technologies convert in-store video into a continuous stream of data on how shoppers interact with each in-store element. The

Figure 17.1 Shopper demographic recognition using in-store video

Figure 17.2 Shopper gender recognition using in-store video

behavioural data are combined with transactional and other consumer data to provide an unprecedented visibility into the shopper decision process.

The measurement platform is easy to set up and the sensors are configured to merge with the retail environment. The measurement process itself is totally anonymous, not requiring any personal data from shoppers. The shopper data are collected in an unaided way, with sample sizes of thousands to millions, supporting a scientific approach for analysing shopping behaviour.

Scalable analytical models and software tools convert these shopper insights into winning marketing solutions. Video-based measurement is truly a revolutionary solution for addressing the urgent need for shopper understanding. It provides visibility into shopper engagement and behaviour relative to exact marketing activation, enabling a holistic approach to shopper marketing.

Figure 17.3 Shopper tracking using in-store video

Understanding shopping behaviour

Action speaks louder than words. With the measurement platform positioned in-store, shopper interaction with brands and categories

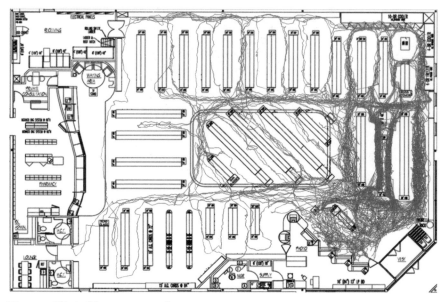

Figure 17.4 Shopper tracks

can be continuously measured to extract a set of standardized metrics affording visibility into key decision processes. The rich shopper data set feeds into analytical tools for quantitative and qualitative understanding of shoppers, identifying opportunities to improve brand and category performance for each market or shopper segment. This can yield marketing programmes that 'listen' and adapt to each shopper segment.

Planning for shopper marketing in a holistic framework

All marketing vehicles can now be brought into one holistic marketing framework, whether they are traditional elements such as in-store location, POP, packaging and price, or new in-store media such as digital signage. Explaining shopper engagement with specific marketing activation is the key ingredient to a planning process that generates a segment-based tactical execution for each retail channel and market segment. With visibility into shopper responses to specific marketing levers, the output of the planning process can create a segmental-level tactical plan that includes specific shopper marketing vehicles. The combination of better models and data leads to optimization of shopper marketing dollars.

Testing in real-world shopper labs

With visibility into how shoppers respond to specific marketing elements, test marketing is now elevated to a whole new level. Testing can go beyond just sales lift numbers, pinpointing stages of the 'shopper interaction funnel' where the conversion has room for improvement. Thus the shopper marketing mix and parameters can be refined to maximize the chances of success. For example, if an in-store POP display is one of the vehicles chosen, the relative placement of the display with merchandise can greatly affect shopper engagement, especially for new products. A recent project demonstrated this effectively, when changing the location of a POP display by a few feet at a mass retailer led to 300 per cent improvement in engagement levels. The engagement measures are also crucial in fine-tuning brand attributes highlighted in the packaging. Further, testing can provide insights into the impact on category dynamics, which is very helpful for supporting retail execution.

Monitoring and tracking the impact of shopper marketing

You cannot manage what you cannot measure. Visibility into shopper engagement and other behaviour attributes allows the selection and tracking of key performance metrics (KPIs) that best reflect the brand's goals. For example, brand strength at a retail channel can be expressed as a share of the category engagement time or percentage of destination shoppers. These brand parameters can be tracked on an ongoing basis to yield a true picture of ROI for shopper marketing dollars. A host of category-related behavioural parameters can also be tracked, allowing the true performance of the category or brand portfolio to be monitored. This enables a realistic picture of the category dynamics, which can be incorporated into retail execution and into the next cycles of planning.

With the fast pace of change in both media consumption habits and shopping patterns, continual tracking of a suite of shopper metrics allows an optimized marketing execution that can rapidly respond to the changing needs of the shoppers, as well as the realities of the retail execution. The shopper data suite from in-store video provides an attractive platform to build and activate brands at retail, communicate with consumers in the store, and transform the retail experience.

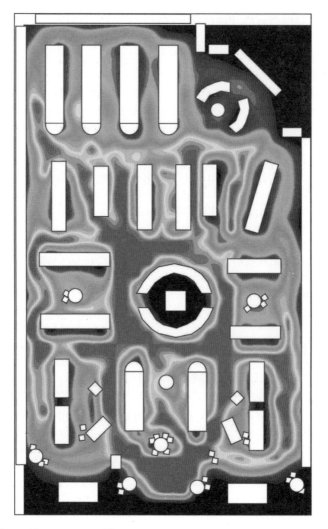

Figure 17.5 Shopper traffic maps

18 The missing link: turning shopper insight into practice

Toon van Galen

A leading expert and pioneer in shopper research, Toon van Galen is the founder of Ratera & van Galen Sdn Bhd together with his wife, Montse Ratera. The company operates from their headquarters in Kuala Lumpur, and helps their international FMCG and retail clients overcome barriers at point of sale across South-East Asia, China and the Middle East.

Fewer decisions are taken in-store than previously thought

People are talking about how important it is to reach out to shoppers. Some say: '70 per cent of all decisions are made in store' (Point-of-Purchase Advertising Institute and Meyers Research Center, 1995) or '68 per cent of all products are bought on impulse' (POPAI). People say brand loyalty has disappeared: '68 per cent of all shoppers are brand switchers' (Nielsen Media Research, 2006). And apparently the conclusion has to be that the store has become the 'moment of truth'.

A massive shift of budgets towards store-related advertising is in full swing. People make it look as if we could wield near total control over shoppers' brand decisions at store level.

According to Deloitte Development (2007), '70 per cent of all decisions are made on the shop floor, and 68 per cent of products are bought on impulse'. We would love this to be true, but it does seem a bit high, doesn't it? Think about it: 70 per cent of all shoppers have *not* decided what brand or product they are going to buy. Do you shop like this yourself? Do you know anybody at all who shops like this? We do not. We have interviewed shoppers since 1997 across South-East Asia, China and the Middle East and we consistently found that the majority of shoppers *do* plan what products they will buy in advance, as well as which brand they will buy; the only element still to be decided on the shop floor is the pack size or variant of the product they intended to buy. Following a series of randomly selected shopper projects we carried out across the markets, on a sample size of 11,840 shoppers, we found that the actual percentage of shoppers who made an unplanned purchase for any given product was only 20 per cent (Ratera & van Galen database of selected shopper studies, N = 11,840, shoppers interviewed for a range of common dry grocery FMCG goods bought in supermarkets and hypermarkets in the markets mentioned earlier in the chapter).

Moreover, the numbers commonly quoted on brand loyalty seem due for revision. We find brand loyalty levels averaging 83 per cent across FMCG categories (Ratera & van Galen database of selected shopper studies, N = 9,794, same markets as mentioned before, average of all measured categories), but of course this still leaves 17 per cent as opportunity.

The effect of in-store impulses is lower than many people like to believe. Another bit of news that might temper some of the initial enthusiasm is the outcome of effect measurements of in-store media. Let us say that shoppers buy, on average, around 25 items in a grocery trip and manage to do this in 67 minutes (Ratera & van Galen database of selected shopper studies, N = 401, hypermarket and supermarket shoppers, grocery items, location Malaysia, 2008). The time needed for the physical exercise involved in getting the trolley, walking the distance needed and putting items in the trolley leaves around 15 minutes for the proper decision process and information intake about these 25 purchased decisions, since we know the average active browsing time per product is 35 seconds (hypermarkets and supermarkets). I imagine you are calculating as follows: assuming shoppers are most interested in information for a certain product category at the immediate moment of their decision in front of the shelf, this would leave very little time for POS impulses to have an impact.

Let us get one thing straight. We are total believers in the fact that the shop floor plays an ever more crucial role in the brand decision process. We are firm believers in the fact that shoppers can be influenced on the shop floor. We also believe that the only realistic way to achieve this is via in-store media. Is it bad if you can convince one in every 50 shoppers to buy your brand instead of another (Ratera

& van Galen database of selected shopper studies, estimate based on the fact that only 20 per cent decide on the brand in-store, combined with studies that show that 11 per cent of those have correct recall and admit possibly being influenced by this particular POS material)? We don't think so. Is it bad that only one in three passers-by in an aisle notice a certain prominent shelf banner, and only one in six recall both the right brand and the message? We don't think so. We just think that we should understand better what is really going on in shoppers' minds and get realistic data about how they are really influenced by impulses we design at the point of purchase.

Figure 18.1 Shopper's shelf impressions

Many shoppers find current category presentations in stores confusing and unexciting. In interviews, the average score that shoppers give for category presentation in the store in front of shelves is reasonable with 8 out of 10 (Ratera & van Galen database of selected shopper studies, $N = 7,469$, sub-sample of surveys quoted before), but also around a third of shoppers find that the layout could be clearer and/ or more exciting. This is probably not helped by the fact that shoppers use at least two competing hypermarkets or supermarkets each week for their grocery shopping and that most major retailers across our markets present the same category differently within their stores, even within the same chain.

A successful shopper marketing strategy has to be rooted in true shopper insight. If, for the sake of argument, we characterize the shopper as a person who has a very short period of time for a decision, a very limited time span for information intake in-store, and a low recall of any impulses thrown at him or her, there is still an enormous window of opportunity. Shoppers can be influenced at the point of purchase even though, at this point in time, the success rate of our efforts might be lower than we hope. Many shoppers also have unsatisfied information needs about products and the suitability of products for their needs. They are interested to learn selected relevant facts about products to help their decision making. So how could we use this insight? We could use a better insight into the shopping and decision process to make product grouping and shelf layout easier for consumers to shop and understand. And we could take away hidden barriers to better purchasing by making the layout a facilitator of a higher-spending and more satisfied shopper.

Translating advertising messages used outside the store directly into POS material for in-store use might not lead to the right impact, since they do not address the specific barriers that exist at shelf level.

Some implementation examples of these findings

Cooking oil case: create a clear upgrade path for cooking oil shoppers

In this study (which we presented at the Esomar world retail conference in Valencia in 2007), we found that shoppers typically bought only one type of cooking oil, and that the main barrier that prevented spending more on a second speciality oil like olive oil was lack of insight into the benefits of using different oil types for different cooking purposes. A regrouping of the category, along with changing the order of presentation of the higher-margin speciality oils to first in the flow, and adding basic explanations at shelf level about the usage, led to a sales increase of 22 per cent (and won the category management project of the year award of one of the biggest Asian retailers, Dairy Farm International, Giant Hypermarket, Malaysia).

Hair care (shampoo and conditioner) case: take away existing barriers in the category presentation

This category is dominated by some of the most professional marketing companies in the world, yet traditional shopper marketing approaches still prevailed in stores during one of our studies. This had led to a traditional brand blocking presentation in shelves, combined with random brand advertising signage on top of the header boards directly above the category, but not matched by actual products directly underneath the boards. All major retail chains used different layouts for this category. A thorough study of the behaviour in-store by shampoo shoppers, which also delved into perceptions and barriers by means of combining five or so different methodologies (such as traffic-flow tracking and video analysis combined with browsing observations and interviews at the aisle but also in-depth focus group discussions), made clear that most hair care shoppers are unhappy with their current choice of shampoo and conditioner.

At the same time they are hesitant to switch brands because of insecurity about the suitability of products for their hair type and lack of clarity about which conditioners fit with which shampoos. For some shoppers the ideal shampoo presentation was a grouping of products by hair type, such as all products for long black hair or dry hair grouped together. Testing showed, however, that this was not acceptable for all types of shoppers, mainly because they did not know exactly what hair type they have. The implemented shopper marketing strategy made some simple improvements in product grouping, putting conditioners not on the top shelf or even in a separate section but directly next to their respective mother variants, and this alone led to a quick increase in sales. The ultimate desire for shoppers was for a quick and efficient verification of their hair type and for related tips about which product combinations would have the desired effect. Some of these findings were later introduced in another market via use of hair testing equipment and subsequent advice on shampoo type and brand, on and near the shelf, with promising results.

The search for the right message at POP sometimes involves breaking the existing category rules

The actual finding of solutions on product layout and grouping, based on how shoppers shop the category, combined with the right message at POP, is an art only a few people understand. Whilst it is fairly easy to come up with a more logical grouping for some categories (think of pet food: people prefer a split into dog, cat, fish, and then divided into dry, wet, treats), for most categories the decision tree is not the right lead to follow when designing the merchandising hierarchy on the shelf. If shoppers buy mainly cheap cooking oil based on price comparisons, the common mistake could be to conclude: 'Let's group it by price and put the lower-price ones first in the flow, since that is what they currently buy.' We may then find that the only reason they buy like this is because they are not sure about the usage of the slightly more expensive alternative oil types. That means there is an opportunity to educate them on-shelf about use of different oil types and thus break the old rules of the shopping process. If shoppers are brand loyal to shampoo only because they are risk averse, but actually keen to change, there is clearly an opportunity to seduce them into a better alternative by breaking with the current way they purchase the category.

Obviously we need to look for alternatives that find a balance between shopper needs and relevance in terms of higher category spending and retailers' and manufacturers' profits. This breaking of the old shopping behaviour rules requires an experienced eye combined with more complex research designs, mostly a combination of various in-store methods together with qualitative techniques and shopper segmentation tools and correlation analyses across various in-store factors.

The road to successful implementations

Even if trade marketing or sales departments find the budget, and the marketing department can overcome the 'not invented here' syndrome and come up with the additional budget and support for properly designed in-store materials, the ensuing sell-in of the project findings to major retailers sometimes leads to demands for cash rather than gratitude for offering profit-generating category solutions.

Luckily there are more and also different parties coming on to the shopper marketing scene – advertising agencies, for example, are starting to see that this part of the budget is not coming back and that communication at store level requires new skills. This influx of brainpower from different angles could lead to a much needed fusion between the knowledge and insight part, on one hand, and the creative design and communication part, on the other hand.

We are no doubt heading for even more interesting times. Let us enjoy them.

References

Deloitte Development (2007) *Shopper Marketing: Capturing a shopper's heart, mind and wallet*, Deloitte Development, New York

Nielsen Media Research (2006) In store ads sway consumers, *Adweek*, 29 August [Online] http://www.mediabuyerplanner.com/2006/08/29/nielsen_instore_ads_sway_68/

Point-of-Purchase Advertising Institute and Meyers Research Center (1995) *Consumer Buying Habits Study*, Point-of-Purchase Advertising Institute and Meyers Research Center, Englewood, NJ

19 Capitalize on unrealized demand among shoppers

Al Wittemen

Al Wittemen is managing director of retail strategy for TracyLocke. He has 35 years of experience in marketing, sales and shopper marketing of consumer packaged goods. TracyLocke is a leading promotional marketing firm offering a full menu of services to highlight brand names.

Sales growth depends on how well you engage and then convert shoppers into buyers. But there's more to it than that. Yes, you should engage and convert shoppers. But you also need to focus on the shoppers who aren't engaged and aren't converting into buyers and understand why that is.

You need to capitalize on 'unrealized demand'. Simply put, 'unrealized demand' is the money marketers are leaving on the table because they've made it too difficult for customers to make a purchase. Getting at 'unrealized demand' requires viewing the shopping experience not in terms of products on the shelf but rather in terms of shopper needs. That may sound obvious, but, in fact, almost everything about the shopping experience today is a function of how retailers and manufacturers do business, with little or no regard for how shoppers shop.

I learned that lesson years ago, when I was selling ketchup for Heinz. Like any good salesman, I did my best to make my numbers. What I discovered was that I rarely did so unless I stepped outside the usual mindset of features, displays and in-store merchandising support. Instead, I thought in terms not only of what retailers needed, but also what shoppers needed. Retailers really didn't care about selling more ketchup; their problem was selling more hamburgers. Shoppers weren't thinking about ketchup or hamburgers necessarily; their problem was organizing a barbecue. So we created a Heinzburger promotion that not only sold more ketchup and hamburgers for the retailers but also made lives easier for the shoppers. And, of course, I hit my numbers!

It all sounds too simple, I know. But that's precisely my point. Creating demand is simple. Unfortunately, most of what happens at retail is confusing, cluttered and complicated. Success at retail is, indeed, all about simplicity. Being simple is part of what we do, and there's nothing simpler than just going and talking to people and finding out what they want and then delivering it better than anybody else.

To get at the issues surrounding the creation of 'unrealized demand', TracyLocke sponsored a study by Dr Raymond Burke and Dr Neil Morgan of Indiana University. This research – *From Demand to Purchase: Measuring and managing shoppability* – was a follow-up to a study Dr Burke published in 2005 called *Retail Shoppability: A measure of the world's best stores*, which identified 10 principles to help retailers improve the shopping experience.

This new study involved a national survey of 3,288 US shoppers, using TNS NFO's online panel of 3.2 million respondents. It also included 'exit interviews' conducted immediately at the end of shopping trips and collected over a month-long period, as well as shopper diaries and information captured directly from register receipts. The questions were: how well are retailers engaging shoppers' needs and converting demand to purchase? How does this impact customer satisfaction and loyalty? What drives the differences in store performance? Which stores are easiest to shop in and why? What else affects the shopping experience?

Dr Burke and Dr Morgan have identified a total of eight factors that affect the shopping experience:

1. *Transparency*. The store is laid out in a logical manner, with product departments and categories clearly identified. Products are organized in a simple way, with similar and related products grouped together, displayed at a comfortable height and viewing angle.
2. *Convenience*. The store is conveniently located, and getting into the store is quick and easy. Ample parking is available, as are shopping carts and baskets. Everything the shopper needs is within easy walking distance, and the doorways and aisles are sufficiently wide.
3. *Relevance*. The store has products in stock that shoppers want and offers an attractive selection of merchandise, including the latest,

high-quality goods. Prices are competitive, and the store carries unique products that are not available elsewhere.

4. *Affordance.* The benefits and value of each product are clearly communicated, with the retailer providing product ratings or reviews. New products are showcased with special displays, which also provide adequate product information. Samples of various products are available.

5. *Convenience/service.* Plenty of checkouts are open, and the checkout process is fast and easy. Employees are enthusiastic about their jobs and are experts on the products they sell. They are also available to help shoppers find their way around the store.

6. *Enjoyment/surprise.* Shoppers find unexpected bargains in the store as well as nice surprises such as new and fun products. The products shoppers want are on promotion. Interactions with other shoppers are pleasant.

7. *Enjoyment/comfort.* Refreshments are available in the store, and places to sit and relax are available. The store offers appealing aromas and pleasant music. The restrooms are clean.

8. *Uncluttered.* Aisles are uncluttered, signage is clear and the store is free of too many similar products.

The point was not only to understand how to convert shoppers into buyers, but also to identify where opportunities are lost and demand left unrealized. Most important of all, when a retailer is hitting on all eight cylinders, the result is satisfaction, which leads to loyalty, which leads to word of mouth, which leads to sales and profits. The most exciting thing about the new study's findings is that, taken together, they effectively tear down the walls between advertising and promotion, sales and marketing and, most important, retailers and brand marketers. That's because the focus is not diffused across the issues that traditionally have divided the business of building sales and profits at retail, but is trained on just one thing: shopper satisfaction. How much simpler could it be?

Think about it. If you have the store environment right, but not the brands and products, nothing happens. Conversely, if you have the brands and products right, but you don't have the store experience, nothing happens. Demand is unrealized. Granted, retailers have more influence on the store's environment, while manufacturers obviously have more control over the brands (other than store brands, of course). But if both parties work together on these eight factors, everybody wins – most of all, the shoppers.

Let's take a look at some of the eight factors of shopper satisfaction at retail as identified by the study and explore where a brand marketer might find fresh points of innovation:

- *Transparency.* Shoppers expect a store to have a logical layout, with product departments and categories clearly identified. They want products to be organized in a simple way, with related products grouped together. Said differently, they want solutions. This is not a new idea necessarily. The concept of 'solutions marketing' at retail came into vogue a number of years ago, particularly with respect to meal solutions. But relatively few brand marketers have truly capitalized on the opportunity to present their brands innovatively within the larger context of a solution. This isn't about reconfiguring categories around the margins and simply rearranging the shelves. It's about developing a deep understanding of how shoppers shop and reinventing categories around that. Look outside the traditional categories and consider creating mini-boutiques around things like special occasions or the environment, for example.

Figure 19.1 Transparency at 7-Eleven

- *Convenience.* Shoppers tend to frequent stores that are conveniently located and easy to access. They also want doorways and aisles that are nice and wide. Obviously, marketers have no control over such factors. But they could contribute to the convenience factor in simple and even unlikely ways – such as improving the shopping cart situation, for example. At many stores, the shopping carts are stored outside, meaning that they become rain-soaked or even icy in bad weather. A canopy for the cart corral – protecting the carts from the elements and fully emblazoned with the sponsoring brand – would certainly be appreciated by retailer and shopper alike. The idea would be a natural for Pepsi, Starbucks or another beverage company, which could also install logo-ed beverage cups on the cart as part of a sponsorship – perhaps including hot and cold beverages for sale right inside the front door.

- *Comfort.* Among the study's findings was that shoppers like to have refreshments available in-store. They also appreciate places to sit and relax. Appealing aromas and pleasant music are also a plus. Last but not least, they like a clean restroom! No big surprise there, but it does imply that restrooms at retail often leave something to be desired. You may recall that Procter & Gamble sponsored something called the Potty Palooza, where they tricked out an 18-wheel semi-trailer tractor into 27 spanking clean toilets, fully stocked with Charmin toilet tissue and other P&G products. Sounds a little crazy, but it was a big success. Why not bring the concept (if not the 18-wheeler) to retail on a permanent basis? Not only would it satisfy a shopper need, but it would also present a highly sensory sampling opportunity!

- *Relevance.* Obviously, the store should have products in stock that shoppers want and offer an attractive selection of merchandise, including the latest, high-quality goods at competitive prices. Most important, the store should also carry unique products that can't be found at other stores. Some manufacturers do customize products for particular retailers. It's not unusual to see a particular model of gas grill or lawnmower that you can buy only at the Home Depot, for example. But you don't see that kind of customization happening as much in other classes of trade. Why not create special products on a supermarket-specific basis? It's a real opportunity to create a point of difference that shoppers will remember. More important, it gives them a specific reason to return to that store and buy your brand again and again.

- *Surprise.* Costco is famous for treating its shoppers to unexpected bargains as well as nice surprises such as new and fun products. But, of course, Costco is in charge of that particular approach to delighting its shoppers. Is there a good reason why the same concept can't be driven from the brand side? I can't think of one. Why not create a schedule of limited-edition surprises to be sprinkled in with your regular product mix on an ongoing basis?

- *Service.* The checkout area is probably the area in most need of help – if there's one area of the store that is full of misery and devoid of innovation, it would be the checkout. Shoppers want the checkout to be everything it so often isn't – fast, easy and friendly. Maybe there is an opportunity for a brand marketer to sponsor a faster, easier and friendlier checkout, similar to the idea of spon-

Figure 19.2 Enjoyment at 7-Eleven

Figure 19.3 Surprise at 7-Eleven

soring things like the parking, the shopping carts or the restrooms. But the other day, as I was watching a woman at the checkout as she unfolded her own shopping bags that she had brought from home, I had another thought. It looked as though it was a real effort for her; she had to bring the bags to the store, stow them in her cart while she shopped, and then unfold and set them up at checkout. Well, what if the next time, she simply returned her bags at the store's entrance and received a voucher for the same number of bags, which she presented at checkout? It would be much more convenient for her, that's for sure. It almost certainly would encourage more people to recycle their shopping bags too. And whichever brand sponsored the idea – complete with their brand logo emblazoned on the bags – would enjoy a public relations coup.

Some of these ideas may be bigger than others. Most are just idea starters. Some might present significant operational challenges. You might look at them and say, 'We're not in that business' or 'How would I measure the ROI on that?' But you'd be missing the point. As I've mentioned before, your metrics – your measure of success or failure – are nothing more than a function of the Burke and Morgan 'shoppability' factors. It is no longer sufficient to take an inward view of innovation, because innovation is not just about your product; it's also about everything that surrounds your product. And the most important thing that surrounds your product is the environment in which shoppers are making a decision whether to buy it – or not. That environment is the retail environment, and the bottom line is that, if you learn how to innovate there, sales, profits and growth will be yours for the taking.

20 The loyalty ecosystem within your shopper environment

Bryan Pearson

Bryan Pearson is president of LoyaltyOne, a global loyalty marketing publisher and consultancy, and ICOM Information & Communications LP, North America's leading provider of targeted lists, data communication solutions and analytic services.

In nature, ecosystems are dynamic. The denizens of an ecosystem don't simply live peaceably side by side; they exist in symbiotic harmony. They benefit, interact with and feed each other. And, to survive, ecosystems adapt to change. Because of these characteristics, an ecosystem is the perfect metaphor for a shopper loyalty strategy in which all customers receive benefits that adapt to changes in the marketplace and to customers' needs and desires.

High-frequency merchant environments with consumer loyalty programmes, such as grocers, pharmacies and convenience–fuel retailers, are perhaps the strongest customer ecologies. They teem with customers, products and purchases, all leaving their imprint on the loyalty biosphere. Customers who use your services every week instead of once a year represent a profound opportunity to redefine how you go to market by building an ecosystem based on insight into your customers' needs as derived from analysis of shopper behaviour.

Given the advances in loyalty value propositions, database design and analytical techniques, these retailers have the unprecedented opportunity to join with their partners in the packaged-goods industry to implement best-in-class enterprise customer-management programmes.

Retailers can develop in-house solutions or partner with an outsourced service provider. Dunnhumby has developed solid practices with Kroger in the United States and Tesco in the United Kingdom; Safeway has a similar programme under way.

Your own optimum path will depend on your organization's strengths and your ability to invest ahead of the curve. To create an information and segmentation structure that makes your loyalty ecosystem come alive, consider the following best practices.

Understand your segments

Every customer-management system starts with analysis to develop comprehensive shopper insights. What are your customer segments and their current and potential value? What profitability drivers will truly affect your ROI? What categories of products do consumers buy?

With most transaction analysis, it's easy to understand who's coming in and what they're buying; more difficult to understand is why. What product and service solutions do valuable customers seek? Can we identify life stages and lifestyle elements by virtue of shopper activity? Does the store format or layout itself reveal activity based on need?

To answer these burning questions, implement segmentation dimensions that make sense for your business model and provide the foundation of relevant communications with your most valuable customer groups. In the grocery space, for example, best-practice companies employ sophisticated proprietary models to determine which items define, say, a 'kitchen connoisseur' segment. What purchases signal cooking aptitude? These models are able to score items according to their fit and value to this particular segment, for example high scores for fresh ingredients and low scores for prepared foods.

To validate this approach, conduct extensive consumer research and market tests to definitively prove the accuracy of your behaviour-based segmentation models in identifying consumer needs and lifestyles. For example, you can use consumer research to demonstrate that the 'kitchen connoisseur' is much more likely to agree with statements such as 'I love to try new recipes weekly.' More importantly, extensive market tests definitively prove that customizing content and messages to focus on relevant products and solutions drives dramatically higher response rates and increases the profitability of direct communications to this segment. This model of testing and analysis has demonstrated real-world success in using customer transactions to predict purchase behaviour.

Continue to test and hone your scoring methodology over time. Because shopper behaviour changes, the best retailers consistently update their models to segment shoppers on multiple attributes that create a true 360-degree profile of the consumer. This life-cycle regeneration keeps the loyalty ecosystem vital and fresh.

Segment ahead of the curve

Expert analysts can take this approach a step further and build segmentation strategies by identifying changing needs, sometimes before the customer is even aware of the need. What offers can you deliver that anticipate what products a consumer might purchase for the first time? This approach creates symbiosis by returning emotional value to the customer.

Here's an example. Maria and Joe are married and are loyal, high-value customers. Every time Maria shops for groceries, her food choices tell a story. As Maria begins substituting her regular purchases with healthier alternatives, you can now identify her as a high-potential customer in the 'health-conscious' segment.

What you can't know is that, six months ago, Joe suffered a minor heart attack. By using needs-based segmentation, grocer A is now able to change the content and offers that Maria receives. She still gets tips and recipes based on her past shopping behaviour, but she now also receives significantly more offers for heart-healthy products. But that's not all. Since you know what other products 'health-conscious' customers purchase regularly, you can now introduce Maria and Joe to additional relevant products and categories that can both drive incremental sales and enhance the emotional connection to your brand.

Enhance the customer environment

Another important element of the loyalty ecosystem is the shopper experience. Is your retail biosphere designed to grow the quality of your customer relationships? Needs-based segmentation offers a solution. Suppose your segmentation analysis reveals a significant index of convenience purchases. The 'time-starved' segment makes up the lion's share of your most valuable customers. Why not design cross-functional strategies to drive a better experience for customers who aren't going to spend a lot of time impulse shopping?

Study how much legwork you require these customers to undergo to make key time-starved purchases such as prepared foods. When someone buys these products, are you making them walk all the way across the store, or are you placing these products close to the express checkout? As you analyse each segment, 'timed-starved', 'kitchen connoisseurs' or even the 'beer and pretzel crowd', work with your operational teams to create product adjacencies that build a vital, symbiotic environment within your retail footprint.

Make no mistake: this level of detailed transactional analysis, customized communications and experience management will increase your marketing costs. But your investment will drive two significant results: strong emotional resonance with consumers, who will perceive that you're paying attention to them, and strong incremental margin per offer.

Who can argue with those results? Within the loyalty ecosystem, needs-based segmentation is a triple win: it creates relevance, builds relationship value and drives profit into the business. Such a retail environment, one that balances mutual benefit and fulfils mutual need, one that nurtures and adjusts dynamically, will elevate your loyalty efforts from mere programmes to customer-centric ecosystems that thrive in the business biosphere.

21 Overcoming common mistakes in shopper-centric retailing

Brian Ross and Miguel Pereira

Brian Ross is general manager and Miguel Pereira is director, consulting and analytical services, of Precima. Precima is a leader in the development and execution of customer-centric retail strategies. For more than 15 years, Precima has helped retail and vendor partners use item-level data to increase sales and profitability by better meeting the needs of customers.

At this point, shopper-centric retailing has been embraced by a broad range of organizations and is high on the boardroom agendas of many more. It is seen as a powerful, demonstrably effective and ultimately essential strategy for any retailer facing the demands of an increasingly competitive marketplace. The challenge now for senior executives is how to take something that sounds compelling in case studies and execute all the practical steps required to make it work within their businesses.

As with all promising new ideas, there may be some missteps along the way. So, with the goal of helping the implementation process unfold more smoothly, let's look at some of the common mistakes and misconceptions that retailers may encounter in trying to put a shopper-centric strategy into action.

But first it helps to have a working definition: a shopper-centric retailer uses insights gained from advanced analytics to identify and understand a core group of most valued shoppers – and from there to predict what might motivate shopping behaviour changes that will make them even more valuable down the road. Responding to the needs of these most promising shoppers is a challenge not just for the marketing group but for all areas of the organization, from merchandising to store design to location planning. This brings us to the most common 'mistake' of retailers trying to make this paradigm shift.

Don't underestimate what it takes

While many retailers can see the remarkable insights to be gained from analysing shopper data, they don't always grasp the degree of coordinated effort required to implement shopper-centricity. A grocery chain will drill down to identify, say, shoppers who don't have time to cook, but prefer prepared salads and meals to go. The marketing team will come up with a programme aimed at steering such shoppers to other products that fit their busy lifestyles. Multiple offers will be tested, all shaped by a deeper understanding of why people buy and what may inspire them to buy more.

Too often, though, there's a presumption that, once an analytical insight points the way to boosting revenue in a category, the entire organization will instinctively align itself behind that goal, when in fact the people responsible for category management or inventory control may follow entirely different models, which can lead to contradictory or misaligned decisions. To carry on the example above, the grocer may have just reduced its selection of prepared salads because of supply problems – so a relevant offer may flounder because there is no operational support to back it up.

The problem here is not only the nature of shopper-centric information requiring new ways of thinking, but also its sheer volume. There is a tendency to generate analytical reports and disseminate them without demonstrating how this data can be used to support the objectives of each functional area – let alone how to incorporate them into existing processes, tools and decision making. This results in half-hearted buy-in, inconsistent implementation and lacklustre results – which can quickly spiral downward into scepticism over the value of the strategy. People grumble about reality falling short of the hype and quietly revert to their old ways.

It is vital that everyone be engaged in rethinking how the organization must evolve to reflect the new focus on shopper insights. People must be shown where the information applies in their day-to-day jobs and how this new way of viewing the business will change the way progress is measured. Above all, senior management must ensure there are clear, consistent communications spelling out objectives and benefits.

Don't think category, think shopper

The shift to shopper-centricity means moving from traditional category management to insight-driven shopper management. In the old world, in order to determine optimal assortment, a category manager would receive a report showing products ranked by sales volume and contribution to profit. From there it was often just a matter of delisting the lowest-performing items. In the new world of shopper-centricity, those financial metrics still apply – but managers also have to look at what products resonate with the best shoppers. Some items that do little for a category's bottom line may add significantly to overall profit, because they play a critical role in keeping these shoppers coming back. Armed with shopper-centric data, management can develop more nuanced ways of measuring category performance in relation to overall and individual shopper profitability.

You can't do analysis in isolation

A large department store, after analysing ways of improving operational efficiency, converted its footwear department – an area with high staffing costs – to a self-service model. At first it seemed like a win: the reduction in payroll and commissions went straight to the bottom line. Over time, however, sales steadily declined. Detailed analytics revealed that the chain's highest-value shoppers were so turned off by the lack of service that they took their business elsewhere – not only for footwear, but also in profitable related categories such as apparel and accessories.

The lesson here is that you cannot conduct an analytical exercise within one functional silo, ignoring the broader shopper experience. In a shopper-centric organization you have to gauge the return on specific objectives in relation to your overall value proposition for those shoppers who matter most. At the very least you need to take a more balanced approach, applying analytics to activities that both enhance the shopper experience and promote cost-efficiency.

The challenge for shopper-centric retailers is that it's much harder to do isolated pilot tests; most initiatives require collaborative testing and complex implementations. But when the result is a more cohesive and mutually rewarding shopper relationship, the added effort is well worth it.

Stop trying to cast the net so wide

Even retailers committed to shopper-centricity have trouble giving up old habits. They continue to apply traditional analytics and success metrics – total category sales, for instance – and slip into the familiar pattern of developing strategies with the broadest possible appeal. As a result, they spend money on low-value and unprofitable shoppers at the expense of those high-value prospects identified by sophisticated analytics. Of course there is still a role for mass marketing. And certainly retailers must offer a competitive market value proposition. But it's hard to imagine a better illustration of the 80/20 Pareto principle than shopper-centric retailing, where a vital minority of shoppers account for most of a retailer's current profits and potential future growth.

So a shopper-centric strategy cannot be all things to all people. It must be designed to appeal, first and foremost, to a core group of highly valuable shoppers. That said, a retailer's target audience may include prospects who are not currently frequent shoppers. Indeed, using advanced analytics, a retailer can move beyond the traditional focus on retention of current best shoppers to create new incremental demand. This is especially true in online retailing, where the technology supports highly individualized interactions via micro-brands, micro-sites and other vehicles. As web-based businesses continue to reinvent historical operating models, using segmentation and customization to personalize offers, retailers may in fact gain the ability to be all things to all the people who matter most – current and potential high-value shoppers.

Expand your horizon – at least beyond the fiscal year

Retailers considering a shopper-centric transformation inevitably ask how quickly they'll see results. When the strategy is implemented correctly, you can expect to quantify a positive impact in months; most case studies show a dramatic pay-out within a year. That said, shopper-centricity is definitely a strategy for the longer term. While a retailer will continue to monitor sales and profitability targets on a daily, weekly, monthly and quarterly basis, these metrics must now be considered against the broader trajectory of a business steadily building more meaningful and lucrative relationships with its key shoppers.

Traditional analytics generate a static snapshot. Shopper-centric analysis yields a continuously evolving picture from which you can make informed predictions. In the old regime, by the time you read a report on shopper defection rates, those defections were history – and winning back lost shoppers would not be easy. A shopper-centric approach analyses current shopper behaviour to spot significant actions – perhaps a break in the usual rhythm of store visits – that may be predictors of a potential defection. You can then move to rekindle the interest of those shoppers, monitoring their response to track success. You're managing shopper profitability proactively rather than simply reacting to shopper trends.

Historically, the outlook of most retailers didn't go much beyond the current fiscal year. The shopper-centric time horizon can extend far into the future as you build predictive models for where your current shoppers are heading, then overlay demographic data on how the entire population is evolving, and think about what you should be doing now to prepare for the changes ahead.

And this, to return to our original point, is where some retailers may be most liable to have a 'mistaken' view of shopper-centricity – or at least a limited appreciation of its potential. Unlike traditional analytics, which focuses on optimizing current business activities, the shopper-centric model is a forward-looking strategy that must permeate every area of the enterprise in order to succeed. Fully grasping its holistic scope can involve a slight learning curve. But there's no mistaking its power to reinvent a retailer's value proposition and remake an organization in the image of its greatest asset – the shoppers it attracts and retains by profitably anticipating their every need.

22 Touching the elephant

Chris Hoyt

Chris Hoyt is president of Hoyt & Company, LLC, a marketing and sales consulting and training organization, based in Scottsdale, Arizona, that specializes in helping marketers quickly become proficient at shopper marketing.

Shopper marketing is today's marketing elephant – not only because of its size or its power but because all of the confusion about what it really is recalls the parable of the blind men and the elephant.

The parable involves six blind men, each charged with touching an elephant and then describing the experience. Each touches a different part of the elephant: one touches the tail and believes it's a rope; another touches a leg and believes it's a pillar; another touches the ear and believes it's a fan; and still another touches a tusk or the trunk. Each has a different experience of the elephant. As their perspectives vary widely, they end up arguing while the elephant walks off into the sunset.

If shopper marketing is the 'elephant', many of the industry participants surrounding it are the 'blind men' – too often lacking perspective as to what it is and yet bedazzled by its potential. Each sees shopper marketing based on a particular experience or opportunity but cannot see it for what it is.

So let's look at the 'whole' of shopper marketing. Best-practices companies unequivocally position shopper marketing as *brand marketing in a retail environment*. They do not view shopper marketing as an extension of category management, customer marketing or trade marketing, although they do see these latter functions as essential to shopper marketing's success. This is one reason why 67 per cent of the

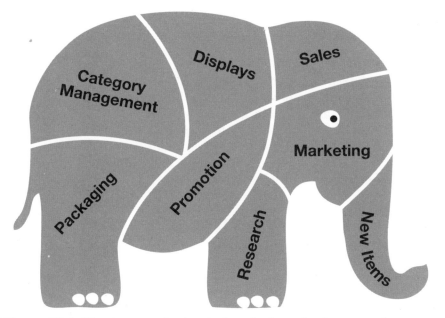

Figure 22.1 Shopper marketing is the elephant in the room that nobody sees the same way

243 respondents to the *Hub*'s most recent survey on the subject note that their shopper marketing departments report directly either to their marketing departments (41 per cent) or to their general managers on the same level as the sales and marketing departments (26 per cent). It is not coincidental that more than 80 per cent of the respondents who noted that their shopper marketing departments report to their sales departments have been in shopper marketing for two years or less. While the sales department is typically where shopper marketing starts, where it ends up organizationally results from enlightened reappraisal based on top management epiphanies that shopper marketing has genuine strategic potential. How so? Let's look at the elephant itself.

The elephant

If we set aside the various tortured definitions people seem to come up with for shopper marketing (including ours!), what defines virtually all shopper marketing initiatives (our elephant!) is one or more of the following *activities*.

Make it easy for the mutual shopper to find and buy one's brands

It sounds simple, but in some environments this can involve a coordinated effort between packaging, environmental design, category management, customer marketing, buying, store operations and merchandising – any or all of which can play key roles in attempting to accomplish this seemingly easy-to-accomplish task. If *you* think this is easy, just ask somebody who markets analgesics, vitamins or hair care – or take a look at any of these departments in any supermarket or supercentre and you'll get the point quickly.

Extend the equity of one's brands through the door of the store straight up to the point of sale

All retail environments are buttressed by communications along a path to purchase beyond the generation of awareness. For nationally advertised brands, the purpose of extending equity is to make use of the awareness that's been built through this advertising via in-store marketing and messaging that will trigger activation at the point of sale by reinforcing this awareness along the path to purchase.

This is distinctly a brand-based function that *requires* the marketing department's involvement to plan and execute it properly. It is in this context that shopper marketing offers manufacturers the opportunity to counterbalance the anonymity of category management (in ways that benefit all parties) by establishing an emotional connection between individual brands and shoppers in a particular retailer. Make no mistake: this is not category management but a deliberate, blatant focus on growing *brands* through brand-specific in-store marketing that uses all of the levers traditionally available to market brands on a national basis. Growing the category may be a by-product of this effort, but for best-practice companies (ie those that are currently delivering the highest ROIs for all parties) it is *not* the primary objective.

Provide a source of differentiation for both sponsoring brands and participating retailers

In our view, shopper marketing for manufacturers is all about *targeting*. It is understanding how one's core target consumers behave as shoppers in different channels, formats and retailers and using this intelligence to develop shopper-based strategies and initiatives that will grow the business (brands, categories and departments) in ways that benefit all stakeholders – brands, consumers, key retailers and the mutual shopper.

For retailers, shopper marketing is all about *relevancy*. It is understanding how one's loyal heavy customers behave as shoppers either in specific stores (or segments of stores) or as specific shopper segments ('brand aspirationals') and tailoring platforms, assortments, shelf configurations, in-store environments and in-store marketing and merchandising to best meet the needs of these segments, eg Safeway's 'Ingredients for Life', Kroger's 'Right Store, Right Price' and Wal-Mart's 'Save Money. Live Better' platforms.

One cannot achieve these objectives for all stakeholders unless shopper marketing initiatives are based on a thorough understanding of how one's core target consumers overlap with a specific retailer's heavy loyal shoppers, demographically, psychographically, behaviourally or, for that matter, all three.

By definition, this understanding should be sufficiently deep to provide a source of differentiation for the development of shopper marketing strategies and executions that are inherently unique, ie built from the ground up to trigger activation among a particular shopper segment in a particular retailer.

Companies that do this well and that have been scrupulous about doing post-promotion analyses and good record keeping are now consistently delivering ROIs of 4–5:1 or 5:1 on their shopper-based initiatives. This is because they *know* what works and what doesn't work by brand and event type in different target retailers and do not deviate from these guidelines. Compare this to the relatively impoverished 0.65–0.75 ROIs that most are happy to get from even the best executed trade events and decide for yourself whether the effort is worth it.

Activate purchase at the point of sale by delighting, engaging and motivating the mutual shopper

Shopper marketing is not just about promotion! It encompasses all of the tools and levers required to *market* to target consumers in an in-store environment – research, insights development, shopper segmentation analyses, advertising, messaging, environmental design, category management, customer marketing, trade marketing and, of course, promotion merchandising – all of which should work in concert to produce a highly targeted result. In this sense, promotion is just the tip of the iceberg – the culmination of all of the groundwork and other activities that will ultimately pave the way for a promotion's success.

Tailor the above activities to align with the objectives, strategies, platforms and protocols (dos and don'ts) of different channels, formats and retailers

Collaboration with retailers is a critical component of shopper marketing and should be incorporated into the earliest stages of planning. Working together to understand issues, shopper segments and motivational triggers simply brings better results. Remember: the point of shopper marketing is to benefit *all* stakeholders – and, most importantly, this includes retailers and their shoppers, not just brands and their consumers.

The blind men

Now that we better understand what the 'elephant' is, let's take a look at the 'blind men' and how they view shopper marketing. Each is representative of a group, and yet each sees only a part, not the whole, of shopper marketing. Consider how those who are contemplating getting into shopper marketing might be affected by how each frames the issue.

Advertising and media agencies

This group is the newest to jump into shopper marketing and, despite its self-proclaimed role as strategist, is unable to see shopper marketing as anything but tactical. Shopper marketing usually is positioned as a new medium in which to advertise (the retail store) with some interesting new vehicles (eg in-store video networks). Few, however, have grasped the concept that the shopper is not just 'a consumer in a store', nor have they taken the time to understand what drives shopper behaviour. Because 'retail' is not their primary business, what most (not all!) of them do is get most of their information on shopper marketing from secondary sources – one of which is the trade press.

When the advertising trade press makes statements like 'shopper marketing, formerly known as trade promotion' (*Advertising Age*) or 'shopper marketing... the in-store appeals that take the form of shelf-talkers, end-aisle displays and the newest in-store video networks' (*Brandweek*), it is easy to understand why this is truly a case of the 'blind leading the blind'. This is from *Advertising Age* (23 February 2009): 'Just what is shopper marketing, anyway? Is it really a form of advertising that takes place in a store? Or is it a gussied-up name for trade promotion or temporary price reduction designed to move product, often at the expense of brand equity?'

Clearly, one is in serious jeopardy if one takes advice on shopper-based subjects from such sources, given their current knowledge of the subject – and yet these are the people with the closest ties to manufacturer top management.

Promotion agencies

For many in this group, shopper marketing is about retail programmes. The good agencies use insight-based understanding of how the shopper behaves in different channels and formats to develop programmes that activate purchases. They understand that the 'big idea' is only big if it is based on this understanding and can be simply and easily executed in an in-store environment. They understand that a winning programme is a win for the retailer as well as the brand and shopper.

The best promotion agencies view shopper marketing as a strategy and operate based on a cohesive plan that connects with the shopper consistently and over time to build devotion for their clients' brands across different retailers. For these agencies, shopper-based initiatives are not a series of disconnected 'one-offs' but all planned within a strategic framework to accomplish specific shopper-based objectives.

Consulting firms

Consulting firms generally define shopper marketing based on existing skill sets within their own organizations and attempt to create linkages between what they know and shopper marketing. Those who have been exclusively brand focused tend to minimize the role that the shopper's choice of retailer plays in shopper behaviour. Those with roots in category management attempt to 'sell' shopper marketing as an extension of category management.

Within this latter group, we are confronted with meaningless terms such as 'category demand drivers' or counter-productive positions like, 'Owing to the nature of the retail environment, all shopper marketing planning must place category before brand.' The fact is that one simply cannot establish an emotional connection with a *category* or extend or build equity for a category. While we have often heard shoppers say something like 'I really love Charmin!' we have never heard anyone say, 'Oh, how I love toilet paper!' Neither have we ever heard anyone say something like 'Let's advertise the pet foods category!' No, shopper marketing is definitely not 'The Next Wave of Best Practices for Category Management' – for manufacturers or retailers.

Retailers

Retailers define shopper marketing as a means of increasing the relevance of their stores to current or potential shoppers. Today's most successful retailers have learned that focusing on customers (rather than just categories), which was originally (for many) a defensive move to combat competitive pricing pressure, is an engine for growth. To that end, these retailers are employing classic *marketing* practices – most notably segmentation, target identification and communications platforms – in addition to their traditional merchandising practices. They are, in essence, learning to brand their stores.

Sales departments

Since most manufacturer sales organizations are incentivized based on volume, it is to be expected that this group focuses on the volume-building potential of shopper marketing – *and* the fact that shopper marketing can potentially bring incremental funding to sales accounts. To this group, shopper marketing means bigger and better promotions that drive higher incremental sales.

A side benefit is that collaboration with higher-level retailer executives on shopper marketing subjects often 'greases the wheels' for promotions or launches. Understandably, most of this group has little interest in the longer-term equity-building aspects of shopper marketing, but this is obviously not a reason to say something as unbelievable as 'Stop relying on brand-driven shopper ideas', as one prominent and influential writer advised recently.

Marketing departments

As a group, marketing departments have been slow to accept shopper marketing. Many reasons have been suggested for this. Among the most frequently cited are: a lack of comparable benchmarking tools; overweighting of advertising and promotion budgets on trade promotion; and a dug-in belief that 'retail' is tactical. Unfortunately, Nielsen's recent decision to abandon PRISM will only tend to reinforce this.

However, our experience is that the real reasons are twofold: 1) lack of adequate research on what shopper marketing is and is not, its growth and ROI potential, and what it really involves; and 2) the reluctance of top management to make the tough decisions that best-practice shopper marketing implementation requires – like telling brand managers that they will have to spend time on customer teams as a part of their career paths and/or ruthlessly cutting trade spending to fund shopper-based initiatives.

While it's natural that different constituencies see shopper marketing as it relates to their own interests, it is important that all constituencies understand that shopper marketing is more than just what they touch. To restrict shopper marketing to one's own purview is to limit the opportunities – not just in the absolute but for each of the constituencies as well.

Moral of the parable

If you are contemplating getting into shopper marketing – or want to revamp your current approach – know the point of view of those with whom you are talking and talk to as many people as possible in order to understand the composition of the entire elephant *before* making decisions!

Reprinted with courtesy of The HUB Magazine.

23 Shopper marketing as a crucial part of retailer partnership

Antti Syväniemi

Antti Syväniemi is head of customer intelligence services at Kesko Food Ltd, having over 15 years of extensive experience in the retail sector. Kesko is a retail specialist having about 2,000 stores engaged in chain operations in the Nordic and Baltic countries, Russia, and Belarus.

Introduction

While markets are fragmenting and individualism has become one of the main drivers of our age, grocery stores are still like carbon copies of each other. From this perspective, it is obvious that the old successful recipe, whereby retailers sell everything for everyone, has come to an end.

Retailers have been trying to differentiate from each other during the last decade, despite the size of the market. Why have they failed? What is keeping the results of differentiation unseen from a consumer perspective? Are identical processes and efficiency-driven optimization with trading partners leading to similar outcomes at the store level?

There is an opportunity for remarkable breakthroughs in aligning the strategies of both retailers and manufacturers in focusing on the shopper, especially at the store level. This could be done by achieving a deeper understanding of the customer's needs and shopper behaviour, and applying that knowledge to create targeted actions at the moment of truth.

This chapter underlines the connection of shopper marketing and the strategic retail chain management process. It also clarifies the best ways to realize the possibilities of the phenomenon of shopper marketing for the benefit of both trading partners collaborating around the subject.

Shopper marketing and chain strategy

The strategic nature of shopper marketing is not obvious from the retail chain management's perspective. One of the main strategic goals in the retail world in the 21st century has been relationship and loyalty building among the chain's customers. This raises the question of whether a pure focus on sales boosting at store level would increase individual purchase, and if so, whether this is in line with a loyalty building strategy. There is no point in prioritizing today's sales over tomorrow's if there's any danger of irritating customers by selling 'too much' or the 'wrong' solutions compared to their needs today. The short-term shopper focus could result in a sales boost, but it might conflict with the attempts to build long-term loyalty.

Shopper marketing – from the strategic perspective – has to be seen as part of the company's strategy and aligned with the chain strategy and management processes. This is done by looking at the whole management process, from strategy building to execution, at the store level. The focus has to be on the shopper who actually makes the purchase decision.

To be able to support the retail chain strategy, the most important thing is to understand it fully. Chain strategies are actualized in the chain's business idea, and the business idea answers the questions: to whom, what and how? A strategic connection to shopper marketing could be found as an answer to the third question. This is done by emphasizing the shopping environment issues at the chain stores. The result of a chain's business idea should be seen in practice at the shop-floor level, through assortment and service completeness, prices and promotion mechanics as well as space allocation and other store solutions. These concrete shop-floor-level issues, linked to the chain definitions, form a solid ground for shopper marketing. This is the point where shopper marketing will be put into action; it allows it to be a strategic differentiation tool by synchronizing segmented commercial and marketing actions to crystallize the chain's business idea in everyday shopping experiences and to generate more sales.

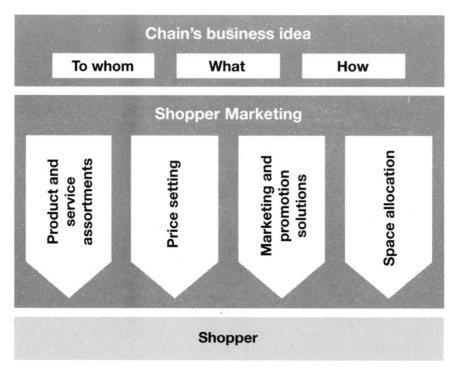

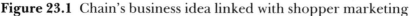

Figure 23.1 Chain's business idea linked with shopper marketing

The crucial role of strategic partnerships

When evaluating the strategic trading partners you should always start by 'walking a mile in their shoes'. Both trading partners should understand what the focus areas are, as well as the issues that are truly generating value to this collaboration. These facts should work as a reminder in planning the direction of shopper marketing. The first point in selecting trading partners for such collaboration has to be the alignment of strategies. The evaluation of trading partners' shopper marketing capabilities follows from the strategic alignment. There's no point in collaboration without common interests, goals and target groups. Only after this phase can the tactical issues be addressed. Could a true common interest be found in customer groups, categories represented and focus areas when considering the quality axis of businesses or brands? A price-oriented retailer is not a potential strategic partner for a premium brand's state-of-the-art shopper marketing project and vice versa. Generally, the 'everything for everyone' approach is not a good fit for any chain or any customer group. A retail chain's business idea is the only relevant starting point for both parties to consider,

Figure 23.2 Strategic collaboration process for shopper marketing

and it is the best way to prioritize trading partners, in order to achieve success, from both the brand and the sales perspective.

The guidelines for this strategic process have to be followed in tactical and operational decisions. Targeting actions for segments, instead of the average customer, requires a deep understanding of customer needs and shopper behaviour. For example, a pleasant feeling and easy shopping experience lower the basic customer desire to shop elsewhere. A strategic shopper marketing plan aims to strengthen long-term customer commitment to the store as well as a product at each and every visit.

Case: Advantages of collaboration in a shopper marketing project

A premium supermarket chain aimed to raise the penetration of chosen categories among certain customer segments. Concurrently, one of the suppliers had launched a new product line and was seeking potential customers. Collaboration was natural based on matching categories, image and target group. The careful goal setting, planning and execution for the targeted campaign was supported by category and CRM specialists from both trading partners.

Collaboration in campaign target group selection resulted in a remarkably better pull percentage. The campaign also increased the long-term penetration of chosen categories significantly. These were the outcomes from a carefully chosen target group and a meaningful offering (ie categories and campaign solutions). In addition, the results of the project made clear the benefits of collaborative shopper marketing (SM) in loyalty building.

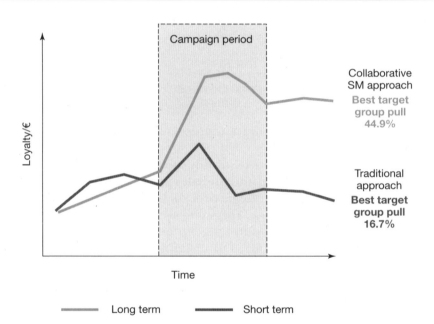

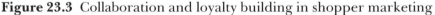

Figure 23.3 Collaboration and loyalty building in shopper marketing

To run shopper marketing in hundreds of stores requires a solid base of information and metrics. Sharing only some KPIs and common information is not enough. The processes, including metrics and information entities, have to be built collaboratively and to be simple enough to make all levels understand it from boardroom to store level. When customers' expectations are exceeded, they tend to rise, and continuous development remains the only option. The shopper segmentations and metrics have to be standardized to make comprehensive measuring and continuous learning possible.

Case: Kesko Food and selected trading partners piloted revolutionary shopper information sharing and collaboration between trading partners

The aim of the first phase was to choose and standardize the early version of customer-oriented segmentations, metrics and analytics to be used for goal setting, optimizing and measurement of collaborative processes.

The second phase of the pilot included various deployments in different collaboration processes from ones concentrating on direct mailing campaigns to others specified for space or assortment changes.

The results from this pilot gave a boost to the development of a new, more customer-oriented retail management system including, for example, re-creation of the targeting customer segmentation. The most impressive results were achieved when partners understood the meaning of collaborative goals, shared knowledge and updated processes.

A shopper perspective creates a need to add the shopper dimension to the information. Required information sources, observation, interviews and POS data as well as traditional methods are quite familiar to both trading partners, but the focus has not been on shopper behaviour. Traditional sales metrics such as revenue, volume, ROI and incremental sales together with marketing metrics (eg frequency, gross rating points and penetration) create a base for measurement and planning. The most important requirements beyond those include the ability to divide metrics for both promotions and different shopper segmentations and shopping occasions.

Conclusion

Shopper marketing offers a great opportunity to influence the purchasing decisions of customers in shopping mode at store level. In a strategic role, shopper marketing has to be a part of the company strategy and aligned with the chain's strategy as well as management processes. At its best, shopper marketing works as a strategic differentiation tool used to synchronize segmented commercial and marketing efforts to crystallize the chain's strategy at store level.

To realize the benefits from this strategic approach, the alignment also has to be applied in cooperation with the trading partners. The retail chain's business idea is the only relevant starting point when considering and prioritizing the collaboration process. Success can only be based on common interests, goals and target groups, and this requires thorough measuring and understanding of the information. Collaborating in these areas and issues is the only way for trading partners to enhance the shopping experience enough to continually strengthen shopper commitment to a store and a brand.

24 Collaborating to ensure shopper marketing execution

John Wilkins

John Wilkins serves as director, strategic marketing and business, for Miller Zell, the integrated retail services firm. The 30-year-old private company provides a fully integrated suite of retail strategy, production and implementation support for retailers and consumer product companies.

Recent years have seen tectonic changes in both consumer behaviour and channels of communication to consumers. Consumers are more demanding, and the number of product offerings has exploded. At the same time, communications have become fragmented. The traditional channels (network television, radio and print advertising) have lost ground to the internet, advergaming, podcasting, and other modes of communication based on new technologies. In addition, the sheer blizzard of messages can dilute the effectiveness of any single communication or campaign, and some consumers may think of some ads as mere nuisance.

It is now generally agreed that traditional media no longer hold the power they once did with consumers, and marketers have recognized that connecting with shoppers in the store at the point of decision is the new imperative. But getting from theory to execution is not so easy – many marketers have years of experience in traditional media, packaging and focus on consumers, but many do not have experience with the behaviour of shoppers in the store. These are very different propositions, and attempts to translate mass messages that target consumers to in-store solutions that target shoppers often fail. There is a critical distinction between 'shopper' and 'consumer'. The importance of this distinction is underscored by research that most purchase decisions are made in the aisle in the store itself – not in front of the television or radio. Valuable influence and awareness are created through TV, radio and other media, but they are not necessarily the final purchase driver. Often the shopper is the consumer. Quite often, however, the shopper is not the consumer. Females with families on average buy soft drinks 2.3 times per week for their families. Mothers are clearly not the only consumers of the beverages, but they are the ones making the purchase decision – they are the gatekeepers for their families of consumers. Developing useful and actionable insights into how shoppers actually translate their and their families' need states into a set of purchases is just as important as understanding consumers' desires. Understanding how household shoppers behave in the store is increasingly important.

In this chapter we are focusing on shopper marketing that is initiated by manufacturers and suppliers to retail, the consumer packaged goods companies that stock the shelves in grocery, mass, warehouse and similar retailer channels – companies that do not directly own retail space but that desperately need to use that space to connect with their customers.

In fact a survey of over 1,000 stores we completed early in 2007 showed that barely a third of in-store communications and merchandising elements actually are installed. For many elements the number is even worse – the survey showed that many elements actually have installation rates of only a few percentage points! This means that, for all the research, creative, and investment in shopper marketing executed by manufacturers, most of the effort never sees the light of day. This does not have to be the case.

Why is this, when 'good' shopper marketing that is based on hard-core research and the development of valuable shopper insights can produce extraordinary sales lift? Research shows that in-store communications, messages and well-designed and planned elements can have an incredibly positive impact on sales and brand perception. For starters, the store is where more than 70 per cent of final buying decisions are made. Additionally, in a recent in-store communications and shopper marketing test in 10 test stores with 10 additional control stores in a grocery chain in the south-east United States, we were able to drive sales lift of certain products and categories by more than 21 to more than 125 per cent at the product level and double digits at the department level with carefully developed shopper communications designed to appeal to shopper lifestyles and needs on a local basis. In exit interviews and intercepts with shoppers in this test we also found that store brand perception enjoyed a significant boost.

Over the several years that we have worked with companies like Unilever, Coca-Cola, Kraft, Wal-Mart and others in the shopper marketing arena we have observed a number of factors that lead to programme success or failure. The number one failure we have seen is the failure of deployment or installation – the issue of lots of hard work never getting into the store.

The challenge of installation has several origins. One of the most important has to do with the incentives that drive all stakeholders to want to ensure that installation of in-store elements takes place properly and that elements are maintained. It is imperative to address the needs of all stakeholders before anything else takes place, whether it is in-store strategy, creative or production. On a practical basis, this typically means that a manufacturer can no longer approach shopper marketing and in-store communications from a brand or product-promotion standpoint alone and must embrace a new model of supplier–retailer collaboration that focuses on in-store solutions that drive lift in entire categories and support category cross-selling.

The one-size-fits-all approach does not work. Retailers are interested in innovation from suppliers that supports entire categories and even supports the development and growth of the retailer's brand. The implication is that the application of shopper insights to the design process must intimately incorporate a retailer's store design, category focus, regional demographics, promotional calendars and general in-store strategy. This needs to be executed on a retailer-by-retailer basis. This approach does work, and in addition to helping drive sales it also has the salutary effect of improving retail relationships.

In one case a large CPG producer we work with created an outstanding and beautiful set of in-store displays that incorporated its support of NASCAR into its seasonal displays. The displays were works of art and artfully appealed to this manufacturer's consumer audience. However, when the company tried to push these displays into use at one large convenience-store client that supported Indy racing, the company's work was completely rejected, and the retailer gave all the in-store promotional space to another company in another category. Not only that – the retailer was so irritated by the supplier's disregard for its own promotional strategy that the relationship was severely damaged. That supplier has since begun to change its approach and is now focusing on creating in-store marketing communications, displays and graphics that respect and incorporate the individual strategies, brand voice, regional and even local demographics, and calendars of client retailers on an individual basis. Early results are very promising at the register.

A key takeaway is this: successful shopper marketing strategies must respect the interests of all stakeholders, including retailers, distribution networks and suppliers. At the supplier level the retail sales teams must be included in the creative exercise with design agencies to make certain that the entire insights and creative process incorporates the people responsible for relationship management. If any one stakeholder does not have a seat at the table, then there is an almost certain risk of creating in-store shopper solutions that a key player does not have an interest in executing or in creating in-store solutions that are off target. If a marketing group has a primary focus on its brands or products alone, then retailers and even the retail teams may not have any interest in installation and deployment, and in-store communications and merchandising elements will wither and die in a warehouse never having seen a shopper.

The key learning is this: in executing shopper marketing strategies, first make certain that all stakeholders are recognized and then involved in the process. This includes targeted key retail clients. Second, make certain that messages respect target retail brand strategies and focus on total category lift, not just brand or product lift. Also make certain that creative respects regional and even local demographics as well as retail promotional calendars. Incorporating these imperatives into shopper marketing strategies will increase the degree to which all stakeholders will work to make certain that in-store communications and merchandising elements actually will be installed and start to drive incremental sales.

25 Putting the shopper into your marketing strategy

Matt Nitzberg

Matt Nitzberg leads the global manufacturer practice at dunnhumby Ltd, helping brands and organizations engage more completely and profitably with their customers by analysing billions of customer purchase records to determine customer purchase behaviours and patterns and converting insights into actionable strategies.

Introduction

Shopper marketing offers great potential for retailers and manufacturers to engage their most valuable shoppers more completely and more profitably. It offers new ways to reach shoppers that can make a dramatic difference in their experience and their spending.

When done well, shopper marketing is:

- an expression of shopper-centric thinking and a deeply rooted shopper-centric culture;
- shaped by a company's commitment to earn and grow shoppers' lifetime loyalty;
- informed by an intimate, household-level understanding of what shoppers buy and why they buy it;
- recognized by both retailers and manufacturers as an area of strategic collaboration;

● managed as a dynamic set of activities benefiting from continual measurement and improvement.

Also critical is brilliant execution, but that aspect is outside the scope of this chapter.

Unfortunately for the industry and for shoppers, shopper marketing is rarely done well. Most shopper marketing programmes and projects have weaknesses in at least one of the areas above. Many struggle in several areas. What goes wrong?

● Offers are irrelevant to the shoppers who receive them.
● Share-of-wallet opportunities among current shoppers are not seen or valued, and thus ignored.
● The primary targeting method ignores purchase behaviour.
● There's a focus on beating the competition instead of winning over shoppers.
● The priority is almost exclusively on short-term results.
● Retailers and manufacturers are at odds over strategy and execution.
● Marketing and Sales argue over 'above-the-line' vs 'below-the-line' funding while failing to develop a test-and-learn approach to optimize business impact.
● Traditional measurements are applied to non-traditional activities.
● Creative and media choices reflect a 'one size fits all' strategy.
● Consumer marketing concepts are reapplied without tailoring to the 'shopper' mindset and opportunity.
● There is no process for continual improvement.

With so many ways to get off track and lose focus, the primary element missing from most shopper marketing programmes is the shopper. Many companies are struggling to expand their shopper marketing capabilities dramatically while relying on limited shopper understanding, outmoded concepts and metrics, and poorly aligned organizations.

As a result, shopper marketing often fails to deliver on its promise. Instead of playing a key role in helping companies earn lifetime loyalty, it becomes yet another way to rent market share from week to week. Given the growing enthusiasm and spending associated with shopper marketing, it is important to understand what separates effective from ineffective efforts.

This chapter will explore the underlying factors that make shopper marketing programmes effective in building shopper loyalty, sales and profits over the short and long term. The structure will follow from the five factors listed above that are associated with successful shopper marketing programmes.

Successful shopper marketing programmes are an expression of shopper-centric thinking and a deeply rooted shopper-centric culture

An expression of shopper-centric thinking

Most companies believe that they put shoppers and consumers at the centre of their thinking and action. But, as the conversation goes deeper, a different entity often emerges at the centre: the brand or the store. To be fair, it is very difficult to wake up every day with the responsibility for growing a brand (or portfolio of brands) or a store (or a chain of stores) without those brands and stores dominating your thinking throughout the day.

These normal pressures make it hard to be shopper-centric, and it shows up in the way questions are asked and answered in the normal course of the day. The questions in the centre column of Table 25.1 reflect the traditional and pervasive brand- or store-centric perspective. If you are ready to move your company from brand- and store-centric thinking to shopper-centric thinking, start asking questions like those on the right side. Asking the right questions is one of the most powerful steps company leaders can take to accelerate change in their organizations.

Several of the examples in the centre column of Table 25.1 share a common theme – attempting to change shopper behaviour through fairly irrelevant brand or store-centric initiatives. This impulse must be subdued, sometimes quite directly, in order to put the shopper at the centre of the action. Here is a favourite quote from a client who urged her colleagues to shift from their brand-centric view and accept a shopper-centric shelving recommendation: 'This is how people really behave. We can't argue with that. We can only decide if we're going to reflect their behaviour in our plans or ignore it.'

Another client confessed that his company spends substantial time and resources trying to change shoppers' fundamental behaviours. When he asked for my opinion on that strategy, I remarked that my colleagues focus on changing our clients' behaviours by helping them put the shopper at the centre of everything they do.

Table 25.1 Brand- or store-centric versus shopper-centric thinking and action

Area	Brand- or store-centric thinking and action	Shopper-centric thinking and action
Targeted marketing	Can we send a mailing to shoppers at the top 500 stores?	Can we send individualized communications to our top 2,000,000 shoppers?
Loyalty	How can I make shoppers more loyal to my brand?	Am I focusing most of my efforts on the shoppers who matter most?
Growth	Is our market share growing?	Is our share of wallet growing?
Efficiency/ effectiveness	How can I simplify and standardize to achieve efficiency and savings?	How can we understand what our best shoppers want and figure out how to give it to them?
ROI	What was the cost per thousand for the ad campaign?	What was the ROI for the ad campaign?
Winning	How can we beat the competition?	How can we win with shoppers who matter most?
Tracking sales	How much did we sell last week?	Who bought what we were selling last week?
Promotion	How well did that promotion lift sales?	Did that promotion engage our best shoppers in the short term and long term?
Pricing	How much will it cost to match our competitors' prices on 500 items?	How can we understand who our price-sensitive shoppers are, the items on which they are most price-sensitive, and the prices at which we hold and grow their business?
Innovation	How can we create a competitive new product line?	How can we create a new product line that is very relevant to our high-value shoppers?
Assortment	Which products can we de-list when we stock two national brands and our store brand?	Which products do our best shoppers need and want?
Shopping experience	How can we revolutionize the way this category is shopped and drive more shoppers to our brand?	How can we reflect shopper behaviour and put our brand where our best shoppers will naturally expect to find it?

A deeply rooted shopper-centric culture

Beyond the powerful step of asking the right shopper-centric questions, establishing a deeply rooted shopper-centric culture transforms, aligns and sustains a business. But how do you know if the culture is really shopper-centric? The same way you understand other business issues: collect the right data and evaluate it objectively.

Figure 25.1 is an example output from a consumer/shopper assessment for a consumer packaged goods business. The company is scored from 1 to 5 on seven different areas of capability. A 'fully capable' company would score 5s for all seven areas. Based on this information – which is collected from a series of in-depth interviews, process reviews and an objective evaluation of the client's ways of working – the largest opportunity gaps are around organization alignment (score of 1 out of 5: 'no evidence' of capability) and shopper/consumer strategy (score of 2 out of 5: 'limited' capability).

An assessment such as this – when completed by an objective third party – provides an important call-to-action about gaps in a company's capabilities, and sometimes about gaps between a too rosy self-assessment and a more challenging reality.

Consumer/Shopper Assessment Outcome (CPG Company)

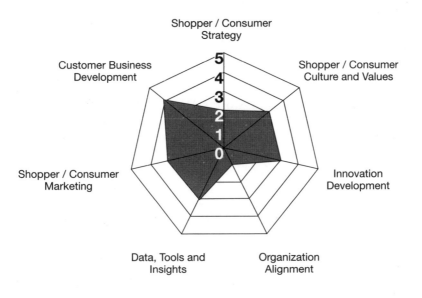

Capability levels: 5 – Advanced 4 – Established 3 – Emerging 2 – Limited 1 – No evidence

Figure 25.1 Consumer/shopper assessment outcome

Two actions are essential to move ahead from the assessment: 1) executive (C-level) endorsement and enforcement of the transition to a more shopper-centric culture; and 2) a specific action plan that creates clear accountabilities across the enterprise.

Effective shopper marketing programmes are shaped by a company's commitment to earn and grow shoppers' lifetime loyalty

Focusing on growing the number of loyal shoppers, and on growing the spending by loyal shoppers, is a potent and sustainable strategy to drive sales and profit. For years, financial analysis has pointed to the relative benefits of growing with current shoppers versus acquiring new shoppers. However, these benefits remained largely theoretical until two kinds of capabilities emerged: 1) powerful data analysis techniques that can tear apart billions of transactions; and 2) the development of new communication capabilities that can deliver fully individualized messages at the household level based on each household's unique shopping behaviour.

However, the value of these exciting capabilities is undermined unless and until a company prioritizes growing with its current shoppers instead of acquiring new shoppers. Tesco is the leading grocery retailer in the United Kingdom – but it hasn't always been that way. While Tesco earns around 32 per cent of all grocery dollars today, its market share was less than 10 per cent in the early 1990s. Tesco has achieved a steady rise in same-store sales driven by an equally steady focus on earning and growing the lifetime loyalty of its best shoppers. This commitment of over a decade is well documented in *Scoring Points* (Humby, Hunt and Phillips, 2007).

Perhaps the most famous of Tesco's shopper marketing initiatives is the Tesco quarterly statement. This communication, which is customized for each household, provides two benefits to the shopper: a financial reward, which can be used at the store, plus offers for highly relevant products based on past purchase behaviour. The statement is so anticipated and so highly valued by shoppers that it's become known as 'four Christmases a year'. The mailing has an open rate of nearly 100 per cent and is a major contributor to Tesco sales and profits because it keeps bringing shoppers back to the store to spend their 'dividend' on the products they want and need.

In the United States, the Kroger Co dramatically changed its focus several years ago. According to Simon Hay, CEO of dunnhumbyUSA, 'Kroger recognized that continuing to focus on attracting new customers meant a lot of money from existing customers was being left on the table.' Virtually everything about its approach to the marketplace has changed as a result of its 'customer first' strategy, which strongly emphasizes the value of loyal shoppers and the potential that remains in these shoppers. Its actions related to shopper marketing have seen some of the most dramatic changes. Table 25.2 shows three ways Kroger's shopper marketing efforts have changed since beginning its 'customer first' journey.

Kroger's focus on loyal shoppers is well known within its organization and among its trading partners, and it's becoming increasingly clear to the financial markets as well. Here's part of the Q&A from a recent earnings call:

> *Financial analyst:* In this environment, you really seem to be widening the gap with the competition. Do you think that you're gaining sales from new customers or gaining a greater share of Wal-Mart from existing customers?
>
> *Dave Dillon, Kroger CEO:* I don't think we try to pinpoint who it's coming from [in terms of which retailer] as much as it's coming from our customers. And, as you know, we target our existing customer base because of the opportunity we see, that in even our very best customers, there are still a lot of purchases they make outside of Kroger and, by targeting them, we have had very good results.

In other words, Kroger is 'loyal' to its loyal shoppers by focusing the lion's share of resources on these valuable customers. These loyal

Table 25.2 Changes in Kroger's shopper marketing efforts

Area	Before customer first	After customer first
Contact strategy	Allowing unmanaged direct mail contact of virtually any shoppers with known addresses	Developing contact principles that put loyal shoppers at the top and creating clear communication guidelines
Investing in loyal shoppers	Not recognizing or thanking loyal shoppers	Recognizing and regularly thanking loyal shoppers
Relevant offers	Placing products on the front page of its circular based on sales history and gross margins	Evaluating every item in its circular based on the purchase behaviour of loyal shoppers

shoppers respond to Kroger's initiatives with even more of their spending. And there's an additional benefit, according to Simon Hay: 'Getting the shopping experience right for your best shoppers attracts profitable new customers too.' Importantly, the reverse does not hold true: focusing on acquiring new shoppers rarely leads to greater loyalty among current shoppers.

To date, a handful of leading retailers, including Kroger and Tesco, have made an enterprise-wide commitment to focus on, understand and engage their best shoppers. Other retailers are beginning to follow this path, as well. For example, the Home Depot is realigning its marketing efforts (including shopper marketing) to differentiate its approach to professionals (contractors, builders, etc) after uncovering that 2 per cent of its shoppers (the pros) drive almost 30 per cent of its sales.

To be blunt, manufacturers are lagging behind these leading retailers in their efforts to know their loyal shoppers and treat them well. They are paying the price for this lack of commitment with high levels of shopper churn and an increasing need to subsidize volume. Below is a revealing and alarming loyalty-based analysis for one confectionery brand. The results and conclusions have been reinforced by similar studies of many other brands across a range of categories.

Table 25.3 shows four shopper segments with decreasing brand loyalty from left to right. The most valuable shopper segment (champions) includes 6,910 households that average 76 buying trips per year in the confectionery category and for whom spending on this brand represents 15.4 per cent of their confectionery category spending (share of wallet).

Table 25.4 shows that the champions spend nearly $25 per year on the brand – about four times the amount spent by valuables and more than 12 and 35 times the amount spent by potentials and uncommitteds, respectively.

Table 25.5 shows that the champions contribute roughly 10 times their fair share of sales based on their size.

When you know these facts, the 'opportunity maths' is powerful and appealing: by focusing on growing loyalty among champions and valuables (22 per cent of shoppers in this example), the brand could grow

Table 25.3 The champions

	Champions	Valuables	Potentials	Uncommitteds
No of shoppers	6,910	125,755	314,501	176,797
Category buying trips/ shopper (annual)	76.1	32.6	33.7	27.4
Brand's share of wallet	15.4%	7.0%	2.1%	0.8%

Table 25.4 The champions' spending

	Champions	Valuables	Potentials	Uncommitteds
Brand dollars	$171,834	$718,381	$612,061	$123,516
Brand dollars per household	$24.87	$5.71	$1.95	$0.70

Table 25.5 Fair share of sales

	Champions	Valuables	Potentials	Uncommitteds
Percentage of dollars	10.6%	44.2%	37.6%	7.6%
Percentage of shoppers	1.1%	20.2%	50.4%	28.3%
Dollar/shopper index	(954)	(219)	(75)	(27)

total sales by 7 per cent through increasing its share of wallet among champions from 15.4 per cent to 18.0 per cent and among valuables from 7.0 per cent to 7.7 per cent. No growth is required among potentials and uncommitteds, and no new shoppers are required to achieve 7 per cent sales growth!

That's a great opportunity to focus spending where it will do the most good. But, despite today's tight spending climate, almost no brand is taking advantage of this opportunity. Most brands' strategies overemphasize acquisition of new shoppers ('grow household penetration') instead of cultivating growth among current loyal shoppers. As a result, the sad story depicted in Figure 25.2 is a common situation experienced by brands today. This chart reflects the year-over-year behaviour of the same confectionery brand shoppers in each of the loyalty tiers.

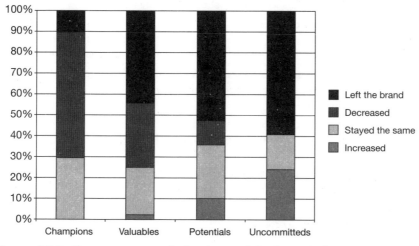

Figure 25.2 Year-over-year behaviour of the brand shoppers

The headlines are that among the champions – the confectionery brand's most valuable shoppers – 10 per cent of last year's households have left the brand, and another 60 per cent have reduced their purchase levels of the brand. No new champions were cultivated. Close to 45 per cent of the valuables have left the brand, and roughly 30 per cent of the remaining shoppers are buying less than they did last year. The largest growth segment? Uncommitted shoppers are growing in response to the increased promotion dealing meant to stem the losses. (By the way, we controlled the analysis to include only households that continued to buy confectionery in year two so that there is no unintended impact from category departures.)

Here's a financial view of the issue:

1. The loss of 10 per cent of the champions costs the brand 1 per cent of its annual sales.
2. The loss of roughly 50 per cent of the sales among 60 per cent of champions costs the brand 3 per cent of annual sales.
3. Net, whatever growth the brand was able to achieve, it could have grown 4 per cent faster if it had focused on retaining sales among its best shoppers.

For those who might still argue there is no upside from marketing to current shoppers, here is one last item on this topic. It shows the return-on-investment for every dollar spent in a well-established targeted marketing vehicle. The measurement was made with a control group in place to ensure the return was truly incremental.

Table 25.6 Return on investment for the money spent

ROI from brand-level offers to different shopper loyalty tiers		
Shopper segment label	Segment definition	Return for every dollar spent (indexed to average for total)
A	Buys brand and brand represents more than 50% share of category requirements (share of wallet)	(234)
B	Buys brand and brand represents less than 50% share of category requirements (share of wallet)	(135)
C	Buys category but not brand; brand has 0% share of category requirements (share of wallet)	(24)
D	Does not buy category	(6)

The results in Table 25.6 clearly demonstrate that targeting current loyal shoppers offers a superior return. The ROI from targeting Segment A (brand loyals) is almost 10 times greater than the ROI from targeting Segment C (category buyers/brand non-buyers).

Effective shopper marketing programmes are informed by an intimate, household-level understanding of shopper behaviour and its influences

Companies involved in shopper marketing need to know:

1. Which shoppers matter most?
2. What do they buy?
3. How do they buy?
4. Why do they buy?
5. Now that I know the answers to 1–4, how can I use shopper marketing to grow loyalty, sales, and profit?

You may be among the large proportion of people who see these three questions and say 'That makes sense.' But you may be surprised by the gap that exists between agreeing that these ideas make sense and actually living by these ideas.

One of the first issues to address is the data your company currently uses to support shopper marketing efforts. If you don't start with the right data, shopper marketing (and other) initiatives will always be less effective and efficient than they should be. Table 25.7 offers a quick round-up of some commonly used data sources and the gap between them and the 'real' shopper who is your ultimate target.

As an example of the power of behaviour-based targeting, let's look at a real-world 'niche' soft drink brand (masked here to preserve confidentiality). In traditional segmentation language, consumption of this brand 'skews' toward households with incomes of less than $35,000. Compared to other income groups, the less-than-$35,000 group consumes 1.3 times its fair share of the brand, based on its share of the population. This is the highest level of development among the income groups. Based on this information, many brand leaders would market this brand toward the less-than-$35,000 demographic via media choices and mailing list purchases. There are two problems with this approach. First, it's enormously wasteful: the brand's actual

Table 25.7 Commonly used data sources

Segmentation model	Also known as	Used by	The 'real' shopper says	Can support superior shopper marketing
You are what you earn	Demographics/ social class	Mass market media buyers and their clients	'I spend very differently from my social peers'	No – demographics are a proxy for how people *might* behave, not actual behaviour
You are where you live	Geo-demographics	'Targeted' marketing industry and their clients	'I can't eat at our neighbour's house – they don't buy organics!'	No – same as above; not actual behaviour and not predictive of actual behaviour
You are what you say you are	Surveys	Many research firms and their clients	'I try to tell the truth as best as I remember it'	No – surveys are helpful on 'why' but not on 'what'
You are what a small sample buys	Traditional household panel	Many retailers and manu-facturers	'I don't see myself in here'	No – sample is small, not directly addressable, and not projectable based on behaviour
You are what average shoppers buy	Point-of-sale data	Many retailers and manu-facturers	'I'm not an average, I'm me'	No – marketing to average drives irrelevance
You are what you buy	Behaviour-based insights	Some leading retailers and manufac-turers	'OK, now you've got the real me'	Yes – behavioural data from individual households

level of household penetration among the less-than-$35,000 group is only 3 per cent. In economic terms, investments made in this group are likely to be irrelevant to 97 per cent of its members. Second, it misses many important shoppers and consumers: while the less-than-$35,000 group is 'overdeveloped', it still represents only 30 per cent of the brand's sales. The other 70 per cent is purchased by other demographic segments.

The solution is behaviour-based targeting. By starting with regular shoppers at a retailer and then segmenting the highest-volume shoppers of the brand, a relatively small group of shoppers who represent 60 per cent of brand sales can be identified and targeted. There is no waste, as non-buyers are excluded from the targeting model. And there is plenty of upside: the brand's share of wallet among these households is only 30 per cent, leaving room for substantial growth.

Behaviour-based targeting is useful and effective beyond brand-specific issues. The world's largest and most sophisticated programme built on the principle that 'you are what you buy' is the loyal customer mailer, sent to 9,000,000 Kroger shoppers every quarter. Each mailer has a different composition of offers and messages based on the prior 52 weeks of household-level purchase behaviour. While each shopper receives 16 offers (12 from manufacturers and 4 from Kroger), no two shoppers receive the same set of offers: 9,000,000 mailers equals 9,000,000 versions. The recipients are the combined set of consistent Kroger shoppers and consistent manufacturer shoppers. Thus they are being recognized for their mutual value to the retailer and the manufacturer. In turn, they are rewarding the retailer and manufacturer with incremental sales.

To get to the 'why' (purchase influences), some leading clients are pioneering the practice of linking household-level stimulus data to household-level behavioural data. Table 25.8 shows a partial list of factors measured at the household level. The resulting insights have led to stronger shopper marketing programmes and other improvements.

Table 25.8 The resulting insights

Household-level influences under measurement	Example	Key questions addressed
Affinity group memberships	NASCAR promotion responders	Does my sponsorship reach my target shoppers? Does it pay out?
Mailed vehicles (coupons, samples, magazines)	Recipes plus coupons	Does my vehicle engage the right households? Does it earn greater loyalty over time? Do I really need to include coupons?
In-store demos and samples	Food sample plus coupon in-store	Does sampling pay for itself via high levels of repeat purchase versus 'naked' coupons?
Attitudinal data (from a 200,000-plus panel)	Needs-based segmentation	How do different needs-based segments buy? Are my segment-targeted efforts working?
Media inputs	TV campaign	Did our advertising appeal to our target shoppers? Did it drive incremental sales?
Brand-owned loyalty programmes	Points-based programme	Do shoppers become more valuable once they join? Are we attracting the right shoppers to the programme?

As media become increasingly targetable to households and shoppers, the insights used to drive marketing plans must keep pace. The only way to do that is through deep household- and shopper-level understanding.

An insight from Edwina Dunn, CEO of dunnhumby Ltd, connects the dots between relevance, efficiency and effectiveness: 'The more targeted the offer, the fewer gimmicks you need to sell it. It will sell itself because it's what people want.'

Successful shopper marketing programmes are recognized by both retailers and manufacturers as an area of strategic collaboration

Strategic collaboration between retailers and manufacturers is a powerful concept because it redefines 'what great looks like' from the perspective of high-value shoppers and delivers on this new vision. It's also very rare. That's because many trading partners are ill equipped and inadequately motivated to put aside their traditional 'zero-sum game' approach to growing their own businesses. How are some retailers and manufacturers getting past this limiting model?

A small group of trading partners is achieving breakthrough collaboration by combining a new level of shopper understanding with an unwavering commitment to keep the shopper at the centre of decision making. The question they tenaciously ask and answer is 'How will this benefit our mutual high-value shoppers?'

When you start asking different questions, you start getting different answers and seeing new opportunities. Table 25.9 gives some questions that illustrate the 'traditional' versus 'shopper-centric' approaches to collaboration. The shopper-centric approach is changing the dialogue and results for companies that can set aside yesterday's model.

While most of these examples reflect the operational or category level, it's critical to establish a practice of collaboration at the top-most levels of the trading partners. The most successful top-to-tops are those where the company leadership of the retailer and the manufacturer each lay out a clear vision of what they are trying to achieve, play back their understanding of what the other party is aiming for, and propose concrete ideas for working together to advance each other's strategic aims – all grounded upon a focus on shoppers and how to win with them. Top-to-top collaboration is also important because it creates an example for other levels in organizations where collaboration has not been a core way of working.

The net impact of collaboration must be that each participant accomplishes more by working together than by working separately or without alignment. Strategic collaboration that includes asking the right questions, aligning at the top and focusing on shoppers will deliver this result.

Table 25.9 Traditional versus shopper-centric models

Area	Traditional collaboration	Shopper-centric collaboration
Shoppers	How can we drive more shoppers into the store?	How can we understand who are our best mutual shoppers and grow their basket size?
Shopper marketing communications	We want you to buy space in our coupon booklet.	We want to invest in our mutual best shoppers.
Category growth	Can we grow 7 per cent this year?	Can we grow 12 per cent by improving share of wallet by 20 per cent among our best mutual shoppers?
Engaging shoppers	We need to lower our prices in the [HBC, etc] section.	We need to improve the shopping experience in the [HBC, etc] section.
Assortment	We are removing 15 per cent of all items.	Let's work together to remove the 15 per cent of items that are least relevant to our best shoppers.
Trends	Let's do an analysis of this trend using household panel data and a demographically representative survey sample.	Let's do an analysis of this trend using your shopper data with an overlay of attitudinal surveys within your shopper base.
Budgeting	We need 10 per cent more promotion support than last year.	We need to know which promotions worked with our best shoppers last year, and what didn't, so we can budget and plan effectively.
Merchandising	We will trade off end-caps between your brand and our brand.	We can maximize sales by sharing the end-cap because your brand and our brand attract different shoppers.

Successful shopper marketing programmes are managed as a dynamic set of activities benefiting from continual measurement and improvement

A dynamic set of activities

Nothing about a good shopper marketing programme involves standing still or repeating activities just because 'they worked last year'. In a good shopper marketing programme, plans are executed, shoppers react, strategies are sharpened, capabilities are improved and new ideas come forward. When used in this way, shopper marketing offers a high-speed, closed-loop learning environment that can improve your confidence and speed your decision making.

To make full use of the many learning opportunities, you'll need to be both bold and humble. Living comfortably with that paradox makes great companies even better the next year.

Be bold: imagine the possibilities that exist when you're not being held back by precedent, habit or past limitations. Take 'We've never tried that' as an encouragement instead of a rejection. Keep your focus on how to do a better job for your best shoppers and you can overcome almost any argument that stands in your way. A reliance on data and insights – rather than making you cautious – should empower you and your organization to try well-grounded, game-changing ideas. Example: a retailer recognized that, in a category with a growth rate of close to 5 per cent, sales could be doubled if it could convince a subset of existing loyal shoppers to revisit the aisle. The question changed from the typical 'How do we grow 6 or 7 per cent?' to the bold 'How could we double the size of the category?'

Be humble: recognize that learning to be shopper-centric is a journey, not an event. Mistakes will be made, unintended consequences will occur, and confusion will appear again and again. Learning to win at shopper marketing is essentially a knowledge competition, and practitioners who are most ready to say 'I have a lot to learn and I am ready' are going to be ahead of the pack.

A few years ago, I witnessed a great example of humility and its link to learning and winning. It was at a top-to-top meeting when the manufacturer's CEO asked how the retailer's learning journey was going. The retailer's COO responded:

We're learning a lot every day about our customers and we're working hard to put it all to use. I feel good about that... about the fact that we're relying on data. But sometimes someone will ask me a question with some connection to shoppers. I'll answer it and later wonder if I was right. The problem is that, since I've been in the business for decades and have had a pretty successful career, I have some confidence in my knowledge and so does the rest of the organization. But we're learning so much that challenges what we have believed, we may find out later that what I thought was true was never true, or was once true but is no longer true, or is only true under certain circumstances. So I need to make sure that I don't try to answer questions that can best be answered by the data we have from our customers. I have to remember that my job is to participate in figuring out what to do with our customer insight, not to replace it based on my personal experience.

Measure strategically for impact

Measuring strategically means measuring what is most important to the business. It also means highlighting what is important to the business through better measurement and reporting.

All commercial organizations have 'outcome' goals like sales, profit and volume. Companies commit to shopper- and consumer-centric strategies in order to increase the magnitude and certainty of achieving these outcomes. If you have a point of view on how outcomes are to be achieved (for example, 'Grow same-store sales by growing shopper loyalty'), you had better measure whether those choices are being translated into successful execution.

The old adage 'What gets measured gets done' is not just an encouragement; it's also a warning: if you don't measure what you say is important, you're unlikely to achieve your goals. If this happens over a meaningful time horizon, you will also undermine your organization's commitment to achieving the goals.

Strategic measurement doesn't just change things within your company. It also changes your dialogue with trading partners. One client at a manufacturer reported that his dialogue with a key retailer changed when he started bringing in new kinds of measurement: 'We used to bring in 20 pages of "what". Now we bring 2 pages of "what" and 18 pages of "who" and "why", and we have a much more productive discussion.'

Table 25.10 offers some examples that link a strategy to strategic measurement.

Table 25.10 Strategy versus strategic management

Strategy	Strategic measurement
Grow brand loyalty	Number of loyal shoppers (trended); percentage of brand purchased by loyal shoppers; percentage of marketing budget allocated to loyal shoppers
Contribute to shopper loyalty growth at XYZ retailer	Percentage of brand growth at the retailer from loyal versus non-loyal shoppers; compare to retailer's overall growth percentage from loyal versus non-loyal shoppers
Create more value for current store shoppers	Basket size; categories shopped; visit frequency
Create a more relevant assortment	Share of requirements by SKU among key shopper segments; sales rate by store type (based on shopper composition)
Launch a premium line extension to extend brand reach and margins	Percentage of line extension sales from non-price-sensitive shoppers
Broaden the appeal of our organic products	Penetration of dedicated organics shoppers versus general market; sales contribution from dedicated organics shoppers versus general market
Leverage communications to drive loyalty and sales	Impact on loyalty and sales from communications to targeted households versus same measures among a matched control group
Drive quality trial via brand equity (advertising, samples, in-store demos) versus price incentives (coupons, discounts)	Trial and repeat rates for equity triers versus price triers; year 1 sales comparisons for shoppers who tried on equity versus price incentives

Measure relentlessly for improvement

Becoming shopper-centric creates sustainable growth because it isn't a one-time event. But, to drive steady growth, you must have an active learning plan. So once you have the right measurements in place, measure and review constantly to drive improvements over time. Figure 25.3 shows how relentless measurement can lead to accelerating improvements. The activity being measured is the redemption rate for a targeted quarterly mailing, indexed to the industry average of 11.8 per cent for response rates for house-owned lists (Penton Media, 2007, as reported in the 2008 Direct Marketing Association Statistical Fact Book):

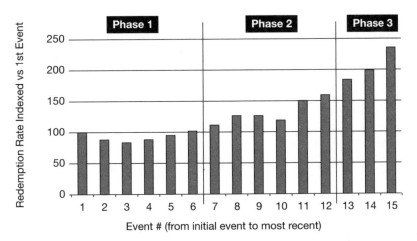

Figure 25.3 Improvement through measuring

- In phase 1 (events 1–6), we focused on getting marketplace experience, building a knowledge base and uncovering early opportunities for improvement. All of the analyses in this and subsequent phases are conducted through a shopper lens.
- Phase 2 (events 7–12) saw the first wave of improvements to the targeting routines to tighten up coupon allocation logic and provide increasingly relevant offers based on past purchase behaviour. There was also learning from a defined set of test-and-learn programmes. We ended phase 2 with redemption results that were more than 1.5 times greater than in phase 1.
- Midway through phase 3 (events 13–15 to date), we have further tuned the offer allocation model to ensure that each household is receiving the most relevant offers out of the universe of possible relevant offers. Redemption results are more than 2.5 times greater than our phase 1 starting point. Encouragingly, the rate of improvement is accelerating rather than flattening.
- Although redemption rates now exceed all relevant benchmarks, we are confident about achieving further improvements. Learning is already in hand that can step-change today's already strong results.

In closing, an encouragement

Becoming a shopper-centric organization is tremendously challenging and enormously rewarding. It won't be easy at first, but over time confusion and disruption will give way to new levels of clarity and momentum. Benefits will emerge in every part of your business, including your relationships with colleagues and trading partners and, of course, in your results. I encourage you to start – or accelerate – your shopper-centric journey.

Reference

Humby, C, Hunt, T and Phillips, T (2007) *Scoring Points*, 2nd edn, Kogan Page, London

Part 3

Execution: what is shopper marketing in action?

26 Increasing shopper marketing profitability with innovative promotions

Markus Ståhlberg

Markus Ståhlberg is the group managing director for Phenomena Group, in charge of the company's global operations. Phenomena Group was the first shopper marketing company to be founded in Europe. Phenomena specializes in shopper marketing campaigns and is the global leader in packaging promotions operating in over 40 countries.

Shopper-oriented promotions

Since the advent of coupons in the late 19th century, promotions have been an integral method for manufacturers to increase sales and gain retailer commitment. By the end of the 20th century, promotions had transformed from a method for increasing sales into a communicational medium. Together with constantly increasing retailer power this posed an array of new challenges for marketers. Retailers of the 21st century are no longer willing to reward manufacturers for communicational promotions that don't seem to have a direct link to increasing purchase decisions or adding value to the shopping experience of their customers or shoppers.

Getting back to basics

The store is a medium that reaches 100 per cent of all potential target groups (that do shopping, that is). For many, this implies that the primary objective for promotions should be to communicate the brand's message to shoppers in a similar way to how other media is used to communicate with consumers. There is nothing wrong with this approach, except that it confuses consumer- and shopper-oriented approaches.

Shoppers are people doing their shopping in the store, on the verge of making a purchase decision. According to various sources, shopper behaviour is quite peculiar in many aspects; shoppers use marginal amounts of time to make purchase decisions and tend to be affected heavily by very simple messages like 'special offer' that would not necessarily affect them outside the store.

The key question is whether the promotions are targeted at shoppers or at consumers. With shopper-oriented promotions, the primary goal is always to increase shoppers' purchase decisions, not to build brand equity through communication. When planning shopper-oriented promotions, the marketer has to evaluate what is the most cost-effective and efficient objective of increasing purchase decisions:

1. penetration, or getting more shoppers to buy the product;
2. frequency, or getting current shoppers to buy the products more often;
3. loading, or getting current users to buy more during one shopping trip;
4. trade commitment, or getting the maximum number of shoppers to the proximity of the product.

In an environment of constantly increasing retailer power, there are only two key approaches to promotions: retailer-specific promotions (for objectives 3 and 4) and package promotions (for objectives 1 and 2). When planning a shopper-oriented promotion, only one of these four objectives should be selected as the leading factor for all aspects of the promotion (ie ask yourself with each element of the promotion 'Does this drive the selected objective?'). Selecting only one objective simplifies the promotion, makes it easier to understand for shoppers and enables you to reach the selected objective more efficiently. This does not mean that other objectives will disappear; they will just have a secondary role that goes hand in hand with the primary objective (eg trade commitment can generally be achieved with all shopper-oriented promotions).

Increasing purchase decisions

Understanding shopper behaviour guides the planning of shopper-oriented promotions. With some simplification, the three steps in affecting the shopper's purchase decision process include:

1. getting the shopper within close proximity of the product (placement);
2. stopping the shopper (communication);
3. giving the shopper a reason to buy the product (claim and mechanism).

The steps have to be gone through sequentially to generate the purchase decision – the previous step is always a precondition for the following step (ie if shoppers don't get within close proximity of the product, they can't be stopped in front of the product, and if shoppers don't stop in front of the product, they can't be given a reason to buy it).

Does the trade love your brand?

The first objective of getting the shopper within close proximity of the product is completely governed by the trade: where the product is stocked in the store, how it is placed on the aisle, where it is placed on the shelf, how many of the product are stocked, etc, and finally whether there are secondary placements in addition to the normal shelf placement. This objective can be achieved most efficiently by convincing the retailer about how the promotion creates value to its shoppers.

Big, colourful, simple

Once the shopper is in the proximity of the product, we enter the marketing stage (the previous step being related to sales). It may sound amazing, but shoppers need to stop before they can make the purchase decision. Even if they end up within close proximity of the product and are given a reason to buy the product, no results will be achieved if they don't stop. The store is the most challenging competitive environment for brands, because thousands of equally attractive products in the same or competing categories are displayed within the reach of the shopper. This is the key reason why so big a percentage of brand selections is actually made in-store. Even though stopping the shopper is often a category-level issue (most shoppers have pre-selected categories they are going to buy but not the brands), there is still plenty that brands can do to achieve this often-neglected objective.

The method for making people notice things efficiently from the complex surrounding environment and making people stop has been thoroughly studied and experimented with in relation to traffic signs. To put it bluntly, are you more likely to stop your car if you see a stop sign or if you see a billboard advertisement? The key thing is to jump out of the clutter. It is not enough to make the message bright; it has to be simple and understandable and above all big enough. Thus, 'big, colourful and simple' is the key guideline for promotional communications that stop the shopper. It is critical to understand that in-store is a unique media environment, and the best practices of other media don't apply there. It is not uncommon to see in-store promotions in which a print advertisement is adapted directly to in-store materials with hundreds of words of text on aesthetically composed visuals. Unfortunately, when aiming at increasing buying decisions, aesthetics is usually a waste of money.

With more and more retailers banning in-store materials, the only opportunity for marketers to stop shoppers is gradually becoming the use of the package as the sole means of communication. When used correctly, package promotions are the most efficient means of increasing purchase decisions because of the 100 per cent store coverage they will achieve.

The reason why

Now we enter by far the most intriguing phase of the process from the marketing perspective. The shopper has, for one reason or another, stopped in the proximity of the product. The shelf is full of products that can potentially fulfil the shopper's need. The marketer has approximately five seconds to convince the shopper to buy the brand. The product needs to stand out from dozens of almost identical products and give the shopper a reason to buy it. The reason to buy the product equals the claim. There are basically three types of claims:

1. brand-related claims;
2. discount-related claims; and
3. promotion mechanism-related claims.

Brand-related claims usually have to do with reminding shoppers about the unique selling proposal of the product. These claims usually gain credibility by reinforcement with launch or relaunch campaigns out-of-store. This makes it relatively costly to introduce new brand-related claims.

The second category of claims, the discounts, are not really appreciated by brand owners, because of the fear of causing negative effects to the price perception of the brand and losing profits. Discounts are also a very expensive form of claims, because they decrease the margins for 100 per cent of the sales volume of the product in the corresponding distribution channel.

The final category, the promotion mechanism-related claims, includes a versatile array of possibilities. The key factor with these claims is the ability to instantly communicate the benefit of making the buying decision to the shopper.

There are two factors determining the core of the claim: the promotion mechanism and the incentive. Promotion mechanisms can be roughly categorized into premiums, competitions, monetary mechanisms and charity, with the corresponding basic claims being: 'buy and get', 'buy and you could win', 'buy and get money' and 'buy and give to charity'. The design of the optimal mechanism and thus the optimal claim is based on the selected objective – penetration, frequency or loading – and on the desired level of investment in the promotion.

Selection of the incentive is closely tied in with design of the mechanism, but it is equally important in achieving the desired results. With the incentive factor, there are basically two guiding issues in relation to the mechanism and desired investment level: quantity and quality. Based on many studies, money is the most attractive prize for shoppers in all target groups. Second and third are correspondingly travel and cars. This brings us to a very important feature of incentives: the communicated quantity and the actual redemption level of the incentives. Sophisticated promotional mechanisms provide means of avoiding a potentially disastrous level of variable costs. These mechanisms enable marketers to give shoppers a perception of a high probability of getting a very valuable incentive compared to the cost of a purchase decision.

To have an effective mechanism and attractive incentive is not enough. The next step is to ensure that the promotional claim is easy to understand and seductive for the shopper, in that order. Another common worst-case practice takes place when the marketer decides that the communicational value of the promotion mechanism or the incentive is more important than its effect on purchase decisions. This leads to coming up with fine-sounding and yet complex incentives, like 'Win the weekend of your dreams in a luxurious spa in Switzerland with daily massage and dinner in a five Michelin star restaurant.' I can assure you that the number of shoppers actually appreciating this kind of message is close to zero.

Innovation means cost-efficiency

The fast-moving consumer goods industry is by definition one of high volumes. Achieving small changes in huge volumes will provide significant results. This also causes the key problem for marketers; you should always aim at making positive changes on volumes without being tied to them in terms of costs (eg if you discount your product by 50 per cent, you are sure to gain a major increase in purchase decisions, but also lose 50 per cent of sales for each purchase decision). This is the key reason why innovative promotion mechanisms that provide high value to shoppers with low fixed costs are constantly gaining in popularity.

27 Nestlé Rossiya, Russia

Lubov Kelbakh

Lubov Kelbakh has been corporate category manager in Nestlé Rossiya since 2006, responsible for category management projects with retail chains in main Nestlé categories (grocery and confectionery). Nestlé is the largest food and beverages company in the world and the Russian market leader in most of its categories.

It is not the strongest of the species that survive, nor the most intelligent, but the one most responsive to change.

Charles Darwin

Russian retailer environment

There are two different understandings of the reality of Russia in the West. First, Russia is a country of mafia, oligarchs, luxury, innumerable resources of gas, oil, caviar, vodka and so on. Second, Russia is a country of poverty, emerging industries, social instability, unorganized trade and a lower cost of living. But what unites both of these is the rapid growth in everything from prices of milk (associated with the state of the global economy) to production facilities and brand varieties. This results in everybody wanting to profit from this situation, no matter what the future outcome may be.

The following trends are noteworthy:

- The Russian food retail market is growing by more than 10 per cent per annum and is one of the biggest and fastest-growing food retail markets worldwide (AT Kearney, including Nestlé internal estimations).

- Consumer food expenses' share is nearly 30 per cent of everything, compared to 19 per cent in Great Britain (Euromonitor)(see Figure 27.1).
- The modern trade share is approximately 30 per cent, with low key accounts concentration and international presence (AT Kearney, including Nestlé internal estimations).
- Russian retail is growing extensively through regional expansion, mergers and acquisitions, and rapid store openings.
- Further retailer competition will lead to overall price decreases, marginal contribution reductions and trade spend growth.

Why do you think that, in a book dedicated to shopper marketing, I've started to talk about growth and economic trends? My main idea is very simple: by reviewing the circumstances in Russia, we are facing the main reasons why retailers as well as producers still have very little interest in learning more about their shoppers. The fact is that the majority still do not even think that there is a difference between the consumer and the shopper. Lots of retailers, when asked who their target shopper is or who they are focusing at, will give you the answer: everybody from 16 to 64 (including children and pets). There is no clear focus for a strategy in the market – it is a one-strategy-fits-all approach. This doesn't mean that it is a failure or the outcome of bad

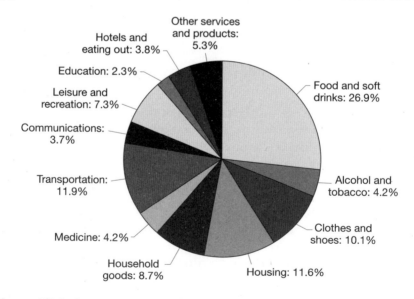

Figure 27.1 Consumer expenses in Russia, 2007 (Euromonitor International)

management – there just hasn't been any need for any specifications or targeting. The current retail environment in Russia could be described as the 'golden age of retailing'. You can easily launch a new product or open a new store and get another 10 or 15 per cent growth. But those who know Western development and are more strategic in their approach will have to admit that it won't last for ever. Some day, just knowing that more than a third of your grocery turnover is coming from families with children under five, or that the wine category is your destination category that drives 'big pocket' shoppers to your stores, will help you as a retailer to overcome the competitors. It's not now or tomorrow, but this future is much closer than we might imagine.

Nestlé Group shopper approach in Russia

Nestlé is one of the first producers that took the shopper-based approach to marketing strategy, as well as to customer management relationships.

Operating in Russia since 1996, Nestlé has always derived its strength from its consumer-centric research. Covering more than 10 categories, Nestlé products were created to be the best in both quality and nutrient value, taking into account the satisfaction of consumer needs as well as their general health and well-being. But that was not enough for it to become the primary CPG producer. After many years of having a limited amount of choice, the Russian consumer faced many choices at once and learned to shop by choosing between different stores, channels, categories, brands and products. That turned out to be another important task in order to continue successful and sustainable growth in the Russian market.

Nestlé Russia has chosen the combined approach of integrating shopper understanding in each business area, from product development to marketing, and ending with a sales team that passes the best practices about the category to its trade partners. It could be presented as a road map of several important steps that are obligatory on the way to best-practice shopper marketing.

With clear goals in each of the categories, the first thing to do is to gather all of the possible information inside and outside the company:

- shopper facts and knowledge in consumer studies;
- information about shopper behaviour obtained from special shopper research activities (from focus groups and home interviews to exit interviews and observations in stores);

- category-specific development in the Russian market that might reflect future shopper trends.

Secondly, it was necessary to get all relevant departments on board to work with the results by finding only business-valuable issues, which were to help the understanding of category development. One of the important players in this process was the channel category sales development department. It turned out to be the centre of shopper knowledge for various Nestlé categories by forming a category strategy for each of the trade formats depending on what and how many products the shopper searches for, and where. Today such approaches generate efficient resource allocation, right at the moment when growth in trade spending is becoming a normal standard of retailing.

Last but not least was to convert all relevant findings into business practices. The knowledge that you possess but do not use is your weakness. It's easy to claim, but it's not easy to do at all. One can say that shopper facts or knowledge is not enough. It is shopper insight that must be considered. We've considered many definitions of 'shopper insight'. All of them tell us that it is the understanding of motives, emotional bonds and even unconscious insights that will help you to get into the heads of shoppers and make them change their patterns. But what also became obvious was that, in conditions of high-speed growth, each piece of information that could change your shoppers' behaviour or each fact that helps you to turn your shopper into a buyer could be evaluated as a business insight. Therefore, in generating shopper added value, it is actions and practical application that should be practised as the only target for all marketing investigations.

Cases and implementation

Real-life examples of how Nestlé proceeded in the area of shopper understanding include the following:

- *Category purchase decision tree.* This is usually taken as the first moment of understanding the category – what consumer needs are covered by a specific category and what factors are important at the point of purchase. By analysing the chocolate category, we've realized that the shopper doesn't choose between manufacturers by simple shelf layouts. By deciding about purchasing in this category, the occasion is the most important factor. The main choice driver is whether this product will be eaten at home with family or given as a present to friends, not to mention small presents for children and also small indulgences for the shopper. Only after that would a brand be chosen. It was realized that a totally different approach was needed. After implementing the new approach in stores in planograms, additional sales were assured.

- *Store layout.* Many Russian retailers, on hearing that a producer will tell them how to create the perfect layout in their store, simply laugh. But after we encouraged one supermarket chain to move the shelf stand in the chocolate category from a very dark and poky corner to a much more reachable place, they were no longer laughing. First, consider the fact that the shopper in this category is the most impulsive (70 per cent impulse) and does not usually go to the aisle specially (aisle penetration less than 30 per cent). Second, remember that in supermarkets the average check for the chocolate bar category is among the largest – which means that shoppers are ready to buy chocolate in there, but don't always do so, because they are not prepared to search for it after a long working day. So, more than 20 per cent growth in the first three months showed that this approach is vital (see Figure 27.2).
- *Cross-merchandising.* It is likely that each retailer knows its own store much better than anybody else and is not interested in hearing any advice. But, when it comes to recommendations about cross-merchandising, only producers who are deeply competent in their categories can advise and help to get additional sales. This is vitally important when we are talking about impulse categories. One of

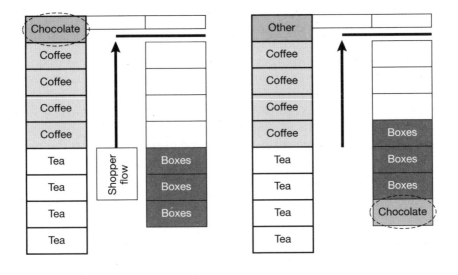

BEFORE   **AFTER**

Figure 27.2 Store scheme before and after – chocolate bars category

these is, of course, confectionery. But confectionery is not the only impulse category. Putting products from one of the dry culinary sectors next to cross-purchased items (for example, fresh meat) resulted in this small category receiving additional sales from buyers who would never find them on their normal shelf. This rather basic example shows that we do not need to change shopper behaviour, but finding out why shoppers do or do not do something can be very useful for a particular category.

- *Shopping missions.* This is one of the most interesting and least developed areas in Russia at the moment. As the retail and the shopper environment changes every year, shopper behaviour changes too. Today we may say that the Russian shopper often makes small purchases. This often happens as a result of lack of cash and fear of spending a large sum of money at once. This is different from the Western type of shopping for small amounts of purchases, where convenience is the main reason for the quick trips. This knowledge helps us to plan category co-promotions and provides understanding about bigger family packs for this or that category in a specific store.

- *Category management approach.* This covers all of the points mentioned above at once. All the facts about the shopping process and the shopper that could add value to a category are taken on board. Category management projects unite retailers and producers to find the next steps for growth based on shopper understanding. This includes everything from category decision trees for creating better layouts to cross-purchasing criteria that can help generate additional purchases. No matter what route is taken, the traditional eight-step model approach or a simplified and modified version, the one thing that should be kept is the creation of additional shopper value that supports additional value to the category. That, surely, comes first from the manufacturers, which have to be the category 'gurus', knowing every single fact concerning a specific group of products. Only that will make them prior partners in such projects. Nestlé supports this type of cooperation as the most valuable, as it creates knowledge transfer to its customers. On the other hand it is the retailer that has to have clear focus to ensure that the strategy is not lost in multiplied targets – so that the loyal shopper can be found.

These are only minor examples of how shopper facts can create added value to a category and put producer–retailer relations on another level. From Nestlé's point of view it is actually the only vital approach to succeed in this rapidly changing environment. It is Nestlé's main task to continue shopper examination at all levels of its work in and outside the organization. Only by putting 'shopper' in the heart of every business area, we can help manufacturers to become 'the species that will survive' and also to prosper from the retail evolution.

28 Using emotional insight in shopper marketing

Ken Barnett

Ken Barnett is chief executive officer for MARS Advertising Inc. MARS Advertising Inc offers advertising and marketing services. The company provides retail, consumer and channel marketing and networking services.

Our approach to shopper marketing is a one-two punch of art and science. That's not a cop-out to make sure all the bases are covered. The approach we take fuses both intuition and truth, pushing retailers further while pulling the shopper closer. We now have to include their behaviours while they are shopping. We strive to unearth the key emotional insight to form a clear picture of who the shopper is as an individual.

The story of Sue

Here's a real-world example of a MARS shopper marketing programme in action. It clearly demonstrates how an intelligent, shopper-centric, customized brand and retailer programme can resonate powerfully and effectively in the retail environment.

Let's start with a busy mother. We'll call her Sue. Sue is the mother of three girls. In addition to her job as a full-time mother, she is also a busy professional for a successful marketing company in Chicago. In other words, high stress. These two important life struggles make her responsibility as a mother more difficult and challenging than it should be.

Figure 28.1 Sue

When one of her girls gets sick, Sue's life gets turned upside down. For her, as is the case for most mothers, getting her child well again is priority number one of 10 extremely important things she is balancing – or juggling is a better term – in her life right now.

At first glance, you might conclude that Sue needs the right over-the-counter (OTC) medication to make her daughter better. Sue is not alone in the cold season, of course. Most retailers and brands simply take on the sneeze and sniffle season by building a huge OTC display of cold and flu remedies in a high-traffic area of the retailer floor. Not that there's anything wrong with that. In today's shopper marketing world, though, it's only doing half the job, because if you dig deeper and push your team to uncover and understand what mothers are really looking for in this situation you'd not only find a different and more powerful solution; you'd gain better, more authentic sales-driving knowledge.

What's just as important to Sue, besides returning her daughter to health, is preventing the germs from spreading to the rest of her family and herself. Just like Sue to think about herself last. This is what we identify as a true differentiating insight – a gem of high-impact information that most marketers wouldn't dig for or even realize they needed to search for.

So what was our solution to Sue's health-care problem? It was to create a display of disinfecting products, driven by a relevant, further-reaching, health-driven message, 'Get well, stay well.' Developing pertinent messaging and visual cues to help Sue disinfect the home, the family car and anywhere that her family could be exposed to germs accelerated her quest toward a healthy home again and, more important, keeping it that way.

'Get well, stay well' (GWSW) connected seamlessly with mothers like Sue, because it was a bigger, smarter idea that went beyond the expected OTC solution. GWSW became one of the most successful programmes to date for the largest supermarket retailer in the United States. It achieved several objectives:

- positioned the retailer as a prominent destination for the cold and flu season;
- drove cleaning category sales;
- delivered a true insight-driven, results-oriented shopper marketing programme.

But Sue's daily challenges are far from over. Besides balancing three teenage girls, her husband, two dogs, her full-time job and keeping everyone healthy, she barely finds time to plan dinners for the week, let alone try to make any healthy or money-saving lunches for the children.

Today she has about 10 recipes she knows the family will eat. They are relatively easy to prepare. All can be pre-made and then baked after work. She struggles because she has no extra time to clip out the coupons she depends on to save her family some extra money. She struggles to find any time at all to search for new and exciting recipes that her family may try and like. Most important, she always seems to be picking up items throughout the week, because her life is on overload and it becomes too hard to remember what to buy. Besides, her shopping lists are always missing two or three key items once she makes time to get to the store.

Her situation is not that uncommon. In fact, it is more the norm than the exception today. What if Sue could go on to her preferred grocery retailer's website and use an application that could bring all of this together for her? She could plan out her week with new exciting meals. She could have a consolidated shopping list to make one trip. She could also pick recipes that she knows the family would try, that would be simple to make and that would provide her with electronic discounts to boot... with no clipping, organizing or remembering to bring paper coupons any more. This type of solution would be steeped in shopper insights. It would solve multiple pain points for her.

Enter the meal planner application. Using technology, the meal planner application can solve most of Sue's problem easily and efficiently. She can use one web-based tool that remembers her, her choices and her personalized virtual cookbook. It becomes her planner and money saver and also helps keep the family dinners fresh, exciting and fiscally responsible. That's all great. But what if the application could go one extra mile? What if it also includes a lunch planner and features a more 'game-like' approach to appeal to those video-gaming teenagers of hers? Her daughters can choose delicious, healthy options and personally plan their own lunches. Their selections are then automatically added on a weekly basis to Sue's master shopping list.

What once was merely a dream can now be an awesome reality. We are currently working with certain retailers to provide exactly this type of easy meal planning tool. Not only will this deliver shopper-centric digital solutions for the busy household, but it will also take it to the next level for those shoppers who want to share their 'new' recipe experiences by rating them as a good addition to their personalized recipe box. This way, it's a win–win, and other busy parents like Sue can benefit together.

The shopper as a hero

To better understand our view of shopper marketing, there is a bit of theory we need to share. Not to worry, this is not about to be a story problem or cause you to hark back to your statistics class. A little mythology reference just seems appropriate. In our eyes, the shopper is the hero.

To create phenomenal shopping experiences (actually, I mean phenomenal) we have broken down The Shopper's Journey[SM] (hope you like it – we trademarked it) to a series of seven key steps in the process:

1. *The awakening*. Before a shopper (remember our friend Sue?) begins her quest, there is a key event that paves the way for the journey ahead. It's when mass marketing aligns perfectly with mass need. Messages barrage consumers from a variety of angles – from advertising, friends and family (like Sue's husband), broadcast and disseminated to the masses. Some of these people, milling about in the mass market, will be ready and accepting of these messages, based on their unique circumstances, needs, wants, desires, etc. A portion of these people, while intrigued, will not be motivated to proceed through the shopper's quest at this time. Those who are

Figure 28.2 The awakening

 buoyed by these waves of messages will heed the call: compelling a consumer to become a shopper.

2. *The call.* The adventure begins with the hero receiving a call to action. This is when the consumer becomes a shopper – when he or she steps outside the masses and becomes an individual with a purpose or goal. This could be a pressing need the shopper is presented with (such as a problem, condition or simply a staple like milk) or an opportunity to expand his or her self-identity with a status purchase like a fashion or technology item. It could be a notion planted by an ad or a friend or by passing something or someone in the street.

Figure 28.3 The call

3. *The crossing.* The hero must cross the threshold between the familiar world and an unfamiliar world. The shopper has decided to pursue his or her quest. The crossing is all about turning those first steps into action. It's mounting the horse or packing the children (Sue's three girls) into the car. It's when shoppers move beyond their comfort level to explore an unfamiliar realm or zone to make an informed decision. It's making the effort to do what they know is necessary either to maintain or to deepen their life or that of their family. Ultimately, the crossing is complete when the shopper enters the store. A separate example is the electronics journey, which mostly takes place before the shopper even plans a trip to the store. The shopper marketing messages and deliverables need and should be sharply focused to support this specific journey when shoppers cross into the space that may not be in-store at all. The crossing may be online searching websites, blogs and reviews. In some categories the crossing convenes in a classic bricks-and-mortar environment.

4. *The path.* Once inside the store, the hero encounters a dream landscape of ambiguous and fluid forms. The hero is challenged to survive a succession of obstacles (brand distractions) and, in doing so, amplifies his or her consciousness (knowledge). The hero may discover a benign supporting power in the passage. Here, shoppers are the most susceptible to brand impressions and the shopping environment, looking for cues and inspiration to help them find the path leading to the fulfilment of their desires. The shoppers' reality is altered, which is an opportunity for an expanded or solidified self-definition that, in this moment, will be facilitated by their purchases.

Figure 28.4 The crossing

Figure 28.5 The path

5. *The reckoning.* Here we have the moments preceding the shop-per's delight. Presented with various choices, the hero lingers. This is where the knowledge and strength of the hero are tested. (Remember Indiana Jones having to choose the right chalice?) The hero (that would be Sue) may discover an ability to do new things or to see a larger point of view. In turn, this leads to the obtainment of that which the hero has set out to find, an item or new awareness that, on return, will benefit the society the hero has left.

6. *The prize.* The shopper becomes fully enlightened to how a par-ticular brand can either satisfy the need or fulfil the desire. The shopper makes a decision and basks in the decision having been made, feeling 'right' with it. The shopper has earned the prize.

Figure 28.6 The reckoning

Figure 28.7 The prize

7. *The homecoming*. The shopper returns home with the prize. There is still that 'afterglow' and excitement. The product, however, must follow through on its promise or else there will be disappointment and bitterness. It's critical to continue the relationship past purchase so that it feels less like a point in time and more like the first step in an ongoing journey. Whatever the brand can do to perpetuate the delight with information, inspiration, entertainment and other relevant purchases will strengthen the brand's promise. The shopper's delight will then radiate outward to friends, family and co-workers. Their acknowledgement of the 'hero boon' will feed their delight and fuel their own journeys.

Figure 28.8 The homecoming

Through extensive fieldwork (see, we're not playing around), we uncovered a cultural model consistent with every good narrative whereby the hero, in our case the shopper, lives with an internal struggle. It's a conflict between 'what I want' and 'what I should get'. The internal right-brain-against-left-brain battle is fought when a shopper is holding the cabinet door open in the store, faced with a choice of a soda or water. And it's fought when a shopper is mesmerized by a wall of sexy, big-screen TVs. The better we understand what shoppers are going through, the better we can arm them with the right tools ultimately to select their prize and feel good about their triumph.

What we learned is that The Shopper's Journey^{SM} is a narrative that lives in each of our product purchases. It could be clothing. It could be a pantry restock. Whatever the item(s), this journey holds true. That's all it is. It's that simple.

We have validated (no winging it here) this sophisticated yet easy-to-understand approach through deep field research that proves people do go through these seven phases. We also hypothesized that, depending on the category, product, buyer, involvement level, cost or service level, the greatest place to have an impact on the journey differs by category or product purchase.

But, as is typical of us, we refused to quit. We dived deeper and also uncovered a series of 'pulse points'. These 'pulse points' are fascinating emotional responses that are likely to occur during each critical moment of The Shopper's Journey^{SM}. Each builds with intensity as the shopper heads toward the prize. If we do our job right (and, believe me, we do), all the branding, messaging, packaging and visual cues come together and the choice the shopper ultimately makes should be exactly the one we wanted him or her to make.

Finally, we wanted to make sure our water wasn't a little juiced up, so we took all of these discoveries to the market and had an independent anthropologist begin dialogues with hundreds of people to validate our findings. And eureka! It works. They love it. They do it. They are it.

So if we truly understand who they are, what motivates them, where they are in The Shopper's Journey^{SM} and at what stage we want to engage them and have the most impact on them, we now have answers to two tough questions. 1) Does the creative sincerely talk to them in a uniquely compelling way, at a compelling point? 2) Does it include the sponsoring product or category? If the answer is yes, we have arrived at our magic moment of impact. The shopper's needs will have been met with a product (brand) intended to serve those needs, and that will grow the category by seeding the sponsoring brand in the solution set for the shopper.

When we unveil that solution for a particular retailer and manufacturer partner, it should be so right that, frankly, it could not work for anyone else.

Is this hard work? You bet it is. Is this worth the effort? You bet it is. Why? Well, this is no longer a world of too many consumers for not enough retail square footage. This is no longer a world of 'If you build it, they will come in droves.' Rather this is a world of 'just for me' – of meeting my needs, at my place, and of being responsive to my expectations. While brands fit that world of varied market segments, the journey people take to get to the brands is different and depends on many factors.

The brands have a world to live in. But guess what? The CPGs are not the only brands any more. More and more, CPGs find themselves working on the promotional and communications platforms or journeys that retailers want them to execute. Meeting these demands will require more work, more knowledge and more creative thinking – but will have a much greater reward in this marketplace.

29 Winning shoppers with cause marketing

Susan Gaible and Carol Cropp

Susan Gaible and Carol Cropp are founding principals of PowerPact, LLC. Combined, they have more than 40 years' experience in shopper and cause marketing. PowerPact is an agency with firm roots in promotions and shopper marketing.

A cause strategy incorporated into shopper marketing efforts will drive loyalty (for the purpose of this chapter, we're defining shopper marketing as all influences on consumers once they pick up their bags and head to the store). We are talking serious loyalty, the kind that gets shoppers to choose one store over another or to drive the extra mile to find the brand they are looking for, even if it's not at sale price. And cause marketing works. We know that 87 per cent of retailers and manufacturers believe that cause marketing differentiates them from the competition (Cone 2006 Millennial Cause Study). Shopper marketing programmes based on cause strategies create long-term bonds to the hearts, minds and wallets of today's shoppers.

Manufacturers and retailers are discovering what many of us have known all along – that the store is an exciting and effective vehicle to affect behaviour. The brand management view of the store has shifted from 'Please don't hurt my brand' to 'Please help build my brand', and retailers are considering their customers more than ever and encouraging their vendors to integrate marketing plans. Taking a cause strategy to the point of purchase can produce huge pay-outs. Here are some quick tips on creating a winning cause strategy at retail.

Find an issue your core customer cares about

Learn what issues shoppers are most passionate about. There are numerous non-profit organizations to partner with, but it's important to pick one that represents an issue that is relevant to the shopper, the brand and the retailer. At grocery stores, for example, women's health issues often make for great umbrella causes to reach shoppers. For manufacturers, it is critical to talk with consumers to identify the programmes they care about. What is a young mother who buys children's vitamins passionate about? Childhood diabetes? Education? Playgrounds for the neighbourhood? And what does the Boomer who is buying walking shoes care about? Is it heart disease? Breast cancer? Alzheimer's? World hunger? Don't make any assumptions about people's interests; seek answers.

When brands and retailers connect to shoppers on an emotional level – through cause marketing – shoppers pay attention. When consumers believe a brand is making a difference, they will purchase products or choose a retailer. In fact, 89 per cent of consumers are likely or very likely to switch from one brand to another (price and quality being equal) if the second brand is associated with a good cause (Cone 2006 Millennial Cause Study). With a fact like that, it's no wonder so many companies have embraced cause marketing. What few do well is to take the message all the way to the shelf.

Be in for the long term and integrate

The strongest cause-marketing programmes are the ones that have two key ingredients: integration and commitment to the non-profit organization over the long term. An integrated campaign requires genuine buy-in from all levels of an organization. It doesn't become a 'campaign' or a 'promotion' or simply borrowing equity from a non-profit organization. It becomes a familiar component of the core message of the brand in advertising, on the package and in-store. The organization as a whole genuinely supports the programme. Its people volunteer their time and embrace the cause as their own. Building a long-term relationship with the non-profit organization is the second key ingredient, because it enables the marketer to leverage the non-profit organization's assets more easily. What's more, the marketer is in a position to seize opportunities that arise as the non-profit organization grows. Non-profit organizations are always expanding their membership base and developing new programming.

Likewise, a commitment to shopper marketing requires organizational alignment for manufacturers and retailers alike. And some smart companies are finding ways for philanthropy to be the tie that binds.

Identify the actionable insight

Retailers now really know who their shoppers are and that they are not all alike. Shopper segmentation and trip mindset studies are driving store resets and prompting new marketing efforts by retailers. Marketers are learning that consumer behaviour isn't consistent when the consumer is in shopping mode. They are revisiting communication strategies and testing new in-store vehicles. And, with new studies that allow in-store impressions to be measured like media, advertising dollars can be redeployed to shopper initiatives. But many companies are drowning in data and failing to use them properly – to drive actionable insights.

Nailing the core insight is key to a successful cause-marketing strategy, especially for in-store communication. Here's why: the shopper is easily distracted. As the shopper heads to the store with the intent to purchase, there are many fields of influence, both inside and outside the store, that will derail his or her intentions. We know that over 70 per cent of purchase decisions are made at the store (POPAI). In our experience, cause-marketing strategies with the right insight strengthen the brand relationship. Such strategies neutralize many of these fields of influence that distract shoppers and keep them from purchasing a specific brand or shopping at a particular retailer.

But not all insights are created equal. Some insights are nice to know and others are actionable. An actionable insight must be measurable. With a cause strategy, the actionable insight is driven from a deeper understanding of what motivates the customer. When developing the promotion, identify the compelling insight that spans across the core consumer. For example, the core consumer might be a busy mother who sees her shopping experience as a break in her day and as a way to entertain her children. The actionable insight may be that she lives in a modest community where school music programmes are underdeveloped because of lack of funds. This relevant insight can be the heartbeat to the cause-marketing programme and can empower core customers to act upon their needs and beliefs.

Engage the local community

Many companies support causes – and many have made corporate giving a strategic value. But few have successfully integrated their campaigns to include store-level activation.

Manufacturers prefer national programmes, and retailers prefer local or regional programmes. The key is to create national programmes with local relevance. The actionable insight must be refined within the context of the retailer. We, at PowerPact, find that retailers want to engage and motivate their retail associates and make sure the programme benefits the local community. General Mills' brand Yoplait® has done a great job of building a national relationship and driving it locally. Their Yoplait Save Lids to Save Lives® programme supports Susan G Komen for the Cure® on a variety of levels and has done for nearly 10 years. It's a simple concept executed beautifully: as part of the national promotion, for every lid the consumer sends in, 10 cents is donated (up to a donation cap). On a local level – on a store level – an additional donation is made to the local Komen Affiliates to benefit women in the local community when the product is purchased at a local retailer. In some cases, retailers honour local shoppers who are breast cancer survivors or local store employees who have battled with the disease. People – employees and customers – like to be recognized in their local community. Retailers and consumers want support to stay in the communities they choose.

Target is another great example of a national programme addressing national issues with local relevance. The company donates 3 per cent of all purchases to support education, arts and social services in the communities it serves – this has been a core part of Target's business model from its inception. Within the programme, the Target shopper has the opportunity to control the contribution. For example, with the 'Take charge of education' programme, cardholders indicate which local school to support, and Target donates 1 per cent of their purchases to that specific school. This allows parents and grandparents to have direct impact on the programmes supporting their families.

Avoid compassion fatigue

The popularity of cause marketing has created a phenomenon called 'compassion fatigue'. People begin to wonder if their donation is really making a difference, and they wonder if they really need to act at all. They become disengaged and desensitized. Just pause for a moment and think about

October – breast cancer awareness month in the USA. Pink ribbons are everywhere. One can't shop, drive or party without seeing pink. Unfortunately, this sea of pink products is tiresome and confusing to many. One good way to prevent compassion fatigue is to develop cause programmes that are transparent and really engage consumers on a personal level.

Safeway did a good job connecting with consumers and letting customers be a part of the cause programme. Its 'Shop & Care' promotion allowed shoppers to accumulate donations when they purchased designated products. That's pretty typical at retail, but what's unique about Safeway's programme is that at the end of the promotion customers were allowed to choose which non-profit organization their accumulated dollars should go to. It's a simple change from having the retailer decide for its consumer where the donation should be made to allowing the consumer to choose.

There are also a number of social media technologies that exist today that offer great ways to engage consumers and allow brands to begin having a conversation with them on a more individual and personalized level. Marketers need more connections because shoppers are only in the store for very short intervals. The rest of the time they are either at work, with the children or online. And, while they are online, there is no reason why the savvy marketer can't be online too, starting conversations that build the brand. There are websites, blogs, social networks, personal home pages, home video, widgets, viral content and more online vehicles that closely connect people to the marketer and to others. When social media are used correctly, the consumer will carry the marketer's message and inspire others to get involved and shop at the right stores.

Consumers don't want to be told what to do to participate in a cause programme. They also want to have input in developing it. Enabling consumers to make their own choices can go a long way in connecting personally with shoppers.

Imagine if retailers allowed their core shoppers who are passionate about a medical issue, like diabetes or breast cancer, to help design a cause-marketing campaign. There is no doubt that we would have passionate shoppers at that store, buying the brands that they care about.

Measure, measure, measure

Don't just measure results. Promote results – internally and externally. All stakeholders need to see progress, and marketers need to see what is working. Measurement must be defined for all parties involved – the brand, the retailer, the non-profit organization and the shopper.

The principles of marketing teach us that the strongest campaigns target a focused audience, feature measurable sales objectives and deliver ROI for the company. Cause-marketing programmes must aim even higher. They can and should be among the marketer's strongest efforts, with measurable sales objectives as well as measurement of shopper involvement, shopper satisfaction, corporate involvement from the perspective of both the retailer and the manufacturer, funds raised and awareness generated.

Among marketers and retailers, sales impact is among the top three factors prompting the decision to adopt a cause-marketing programme (PowerPact 2004 Cause Marketing Study). If a marketing programme doesn't meet specific sales objectives, the sponsor won't turn a profit. If a sponsor doesn't make a profit, it won't achieve the budgets it deserves and ultimately will not generate the awareness, constituent base and shopper-driven dollars that worthy non-profit organizations need in order to prosper.

Allow your programme to evolve

Don't be afraid to change. The best programmes are nimble. With new technology, and with new studies on the impact of digital media on the shopping process, it is critical that programmes adjust to new learning. Test, learn and adjust.

With Web 2.0 and consumer adaptation of new media and the use of mobile technology in the retail environment, testing is even more important. One great way to see how a programme is doing is to listen to customers online. We suggest reading and participating in private forums or blogs. Find a blog or start one, with people who care about a specific store or product. The result is valuable insights about what the most vocal consumers think about the store, the brand and the charities and non-profit organizations you and they support.

Winning shoppers with cause marketing

- Find an issue your core customer cares about.
- Be in for the long term and integrate.
- Identify the actionable insight.
- Engage the local community.
- Avoid compassion fatigue.
- Measure, measure, measure.
- Allow your programme to evolve.

We are passionate about integrating cause-marketing strategies into shopper behaviour, and we know what it takes to reach the hearts, minds and wallets of today's shoppers. We can't promise more foot traffic, more frequent shopping or more consumer effort spent to get to the right stores. We don't guarantee how often shoppers will tell their friends and family that 'This is the place to shop.' But we know from successful experience that these seven tips produce cause-based marketing programmes that bring the brand, the store, the cause and the consumer together passionately for common purpose and maximum benefit.

30 Tesco Fresh & Easy, USA

Simon Uwins

Simon Uwins is chief marketing officer of Tesco's Fresh & Easy Neighborhood Market. Simon ran Tesco's bakery, health/beauty and non-foods categories prior to leading its marketing in the United Kingdom. Tesco is a British-based international grocery and general merchandising retail chain. It is the largest British retailer by both global sales and domestic market share.

Working for a major food retailer, I find the recent rise in popularity of shopper marketing a little strange. Why? Because the shopping trip has always been so central to our business. After all, what people think about our brand is almost exclusively based on their experience of their local store.

If you accept that a brand is simply an associative network of emotional, sensory and rational experiences in our memory, all these elements come together day in, day out in a shopping trip. And, as we are a food retailer, people shop with us frequently.

We focus on ensuring that our shopping trip creates value for customers every day, so that they want to shop with us again and again. And we try to bring together all the shopping trip's elements coherently, so that it communicates what the brand is about. Fresh & Easy Neighborhood Market, the business we've established in the southwest United States, was built on these principles.

Creating value for customers

Our initial step was to find out what would create enough value for customers, so that they would want to shop with us. We had an idea.

Across many markets we were seeing the development of smaller food stores, which fit better into people's busy lives. But we noticed that, in the United States, it didn't seem to be happening. So we set out to understand whether or not it was of value to people there.

We used a variety of techniques (I've always found the most reliable insights come from triangulating results from several sources). Focus groups were a start, but we needed to confront people with the reality of their behaviour, to get richer and more accurate insights. We went into people's homes, interviewed them around their attitude to food, food preparation and food shopping habits. We had a look in their refrigerators, freezers, pantries and anywhere else they stored food – including, in many cases, the garage! This served to remind people of other stores they had shopped in, and the kinds of foods they were really eating.

Of course, to really understand how people shop, there's no substitute for going shopping with them, so we did, sometimes just observing them as shoppers, sometimes talking to them about how they approach a particular area. For example, we asked people to buy the worst meat and the best meat on display in a number of different retailers and then explain why they chose what they chose.

Although we were talking to people from all types of backgrounds, we found a remarkable consistency among them:

- They wanted the convenience of shopping locally, but they felt they had to shop in many different stores in order to get everything they wanted.
- They had a feeling that something wasn't quite right about the food they were being offered, so they were going in search of fresher, more wholesome, authentic food if they could afford it.
- They felt their local supermarkets were generally expensive, so they were visiting a variety of stores to stretch their budget, often buying just on deal.
- The shopping trips themselves were not particularly easy. They often found it difficult to find what they wanted, as there were so many similar products on display, often in multiple locations. Prices at the shelf edge could be quite confusing, and they resented having to carry so many loyalty cards to get lower prices. They felt they often had to wait in line, even when a store wasn't busy. They also found stores, with some notable exceptions, unfriendly places.

To understand what kind of shopping trip might fit them better, we did a series of exercises both group and individual, where we got people to describe their ideal shopping trip. Again, what we heard was remarkably consistent:

- a store that sold fresh, wholesome food but where you could also get all your regular products;
- a store that was affordable, with honest low prices for everybody;
- a store that was quick to get in and out of;
- a store that was friendly and treated you as a person.

So we designed a store to deliver this. It would be relatively small, about 10,000 square feet, laid out in a logical sequence to make it easy to shop. It would carry only 3,500 products but by careful editing still enable people to get everything they wanted, with a strong emphasis on fresh, wholesome and convenient food. It would have a new type of assisted checkout operation, so that every checkout would be open all the time. And it would be simple to operate, so that prices could be kept low.

Of course, we had to make sure that we interpreted all this insight correctly, so that it would create enough value for people to want to shop with us. We built a full-scale prototype inside a warehouse, stocked it with representative products and invited people to come and shop in it. We found we'd got it more right than wrong – Fresh & Easy Neighborhood Market was born.

Figure 30.1 Tesco Fresh & Easy Henderson

Communicating through the shopping trip

As I noted earlier, a shopping trip is a living, breathing entity that communicates what the brand is about in sensory and emotional, as well as rational, ways. Indeed it's no different to the way we communicate with each other: a bit is what we say, a bit is how we say it, but mostly it's our body language. So in developing the Fresh & Easy shopping trip, we paid a lot of attention to ensuring it communicates what people told us they valued.

As far as what we say is concerned, we set out to make clear the principles behind the shopping trip and then to provide information around the store that demonstrated we were delivering against them. For example, written large on one of the walls of our stores is our belief that everyone deserves quality food they can trust. Around the store you'll find information pointing out that all of our Fresh & Easy brand products contain no artificial colours or flavours, no added transfats and, except where absolutely necessary, no artificial preservatives – factual evidence of our belief in action.

In terms of how we say it, our tone is honest, straightforward and conversational, as if we're talking face to face. We're just people, after all, so why not talk that way?

Getting your body language right is by far the most difficult. As a start, we went through every element of the shopping trip, to bring it into line. For example, since we are offering fresher, more wholesome food, our packaging simply lets you see the product, where it's technically possible, so you can judge for yourself – why cover the product up, put a photograph on the front, and then try to convince people how fresh and wholesome the product is? To ensure it's quick and easy to shop, we make sure the aisles are wide and uncluttered, the shelf heights lower so you can see across the store, and the only hanging signage used simply points out where things are. And, since our prices are low, at the shelf edge the price of a product is extremely clear, and our fixturization simple.

Being a store that's friendly is the hardest of all. Your tone of written communication around the store can be conversational, and you can stick a neighbourhood notice board on the wall. But it's really all about the people who work in it and how they interact with each other and their customers. One of the best insights we got was around this. We found people were very clear about which stores gave great service. They weren't the ones with the most service counters or employees on the shop floor. They were the stores where the employees are friendly, treating their customers as real people. What made the difference? It was obvious to them – these were stores where people enjoyed working. So we've gone to great lengths to create a workplace that people can enjoy. We used the same approach as in developing the shopping trip – talking to people in a variety of ways, this time about what makes a great place to work and then setting out to deliver it.

An organizational endeavour

The fact that you need to create a great place to work in order to have friendly stores underlines a fundamental point: shopper marketing from a retailer's point of view is not something that can simply be grafted on at the end.

Once you've worked out what shopping trip will create enough value for people to want to shop with you and how to reinforce that value through coherent communication, you need to build the organizational capability to deliver it. In other words, you need to work backwards from the shelf edge.

Take the example of providing fresher, more wholesome food. This isn't just a clever piece of marketing. You need to be able to deliver it. Based upon what we heard, we put in place a policy that no Fresh & Easy brand product should contain artificial colours or flavours or added transfats, and they should use preservatives only where absolutely necessary. This meant that our buyers and food technologists had to find suppliers capable of doing this, and work with them to achieve it. Indeed, in the case of fresh prepared meals, we ended up building our own kitchen facility, to exacting standards.

Or take the example of low prices. To enable them to be surprisingly low in our customers' eyes, we had to make our operating model extremely simple, to keep costs low. From day one, for example, all our products were delivered in display-ready packaging, to save time putting them on the shelf.

Of course, a shopping trip is a living, breathing entity involving many, many interactions every day, in multiple locations. You can't hope to control it. So we've tried to embed it into the organization's DNA, by building the values of the organization around it. These describe the kinds of shopping trip we're trying to offer, and the kind of business we're trying to be. We've made them central to everybody's job description, so it's a joint endeavour.

Quite how successful Fresh & Easy will become it's far too early to judge. What is certain is that it's inspiring a degree of customer satisfaction and recommendation that's highly unusual in the food retailing arena. For a retail marketer, shopper marketing is not about influencing purchase decisions close to the product in the store. It's about ensuring that your customers want to shop with you today, tomorrow, next week and next year. And that, in my view, is how it should be.

31 Shopper-oriented pricing strategies

Jon Hauptman

Jon Hauptman leads Willard Bishop's retail pricing strategy and shopper marketing practice areas. Willard Bishop provides marketing strategies and data modelling to improve the retail consumer experience.

Price is becoming an increasingly important driver of store choice, as many parts of the world are experiencing extremely high food price inflation, an economic downturn or both. In this environment, shoppers are looking more closely at available retail options and choosing to shop in those stores with the strongest price image, ie where they believe they can stretch their grocery dollars the most.

In turn, retailers are searching for ways to enhance their price image while attracting more shopper visits, improving shopper loyalty and driving sales growth – profitably. Progressive retailers have done this successfully by developing and implementing shopper-oriented pricing strategies based on two fundamental concepts: 1) understanding and managing 'pricing tipping points'; and 2) strengthening each of the 'six dimensions of price image'.

Following is a more complete description of these concepts and how retailers are leveraging them to enhance price image.

Pricing tipping points: managing price gaps based on shopper perceptions

Pricing tipping points represent a new way for retailers to manage price image efficiently and effectively in today's increasingly competitive marketplace. They represent the maximum price gap shoppers will tolerate before shifting their spending to other stores. The exact levels are based on the actual prices shoppers see in the store, combined with their experiences and satisfaction with all other elements of the value equation, eg location, assortment, quality, service and so on.

To compete effectively, supermarkets don't have to match competitor prices. Instead, they can identify and manage their tipping points by examining shopper perceptions of – and tolerance for – price gaps among retailers.

Shopper perceptions of total store price differentials

Shopper perceptions of price differentials among retailers fall into three zones:

1. *Imperceptible.* There's a long-standing myth that a retailer has to match competitor prices to be considered 'at parity'. But, typically, shoppers don't notice small differences in the total store prices between two retailers. So a retailer doesn't gain much by setting total store prices just slightly below those of a key competitor. On the other hand, if a retailer wants to maintain a 'parity' price position versus a competitor, it can strategically set selected prices a little higher than those of its key competitor without negatively affecting its price image.
2. *Perceptible.* There is, however, a point at which shoppers begin to recognize price differences between two retailers, ie in the 'perceptible' zone. At this point, shoppers may not leave their preferred stores if they perceive the prices to be a little higher, but they do notice. A retailer's ability to differentiate meaningfully versus competitors in other areas of the value equation (variety, quality, service, etc) is what retains shoppers, despite the acknowledged price gap. This represents the premium that shoppers are willing to pay providing their store offers something they highly value above and beyond 'price'.
3. *Significant.* However, the premium that most shoppers are willing to pay is not infinite. There is also a point at which price dominates shopper store choice decisions: it's called 'the tipping point'. This is where price gaps are so large that they shift shopper perceptions from the 'perceptible' (but tolerable) zone into the 'significant' zone, and this causes shoppers to shift spending to other stores with more attractive value propositions.

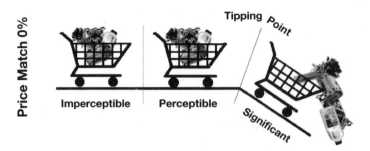

Figure 31.1 Shopper perceptions of total store price differentials

Actual tipping points vary by retailer, depending on each retailer's strengths versus those of key competitors. For example, in a recent study of a large Midwest US market, two retailers exhibit very different tipping points. One retailer, an upscale supermarket operator, enjoys a tipping point of approximately 10 per cent, ie it is successfully maintaining a 10 per cent total store price premium versus its leading competitor, owing to the power of its non-price offering, eg service, perishables and unique variety. In the same market, a second retailer – a traditional supermarket chain – found that it could maintain a tipping point of only 5 per cent versus the same key competitor. Its non-price offering was not superior enough to have earned more.

Six dimensions of price image: the building blocks of a shopper-oriented pricing strategy

Shoppers generate their price image of a store through their experiences in each of 'six dimensions'. These dimensions are similar to the links in a six-link chain, where weakness in one link compromises the strength of the entire chain; similarly, weakness in only one dimension can adversely affect shopper price image of a store. Consequently, a strong and successful price image requires a strong offering in each of the six dimensions, and the most effective pricing strategies provide direction and solutions to managing each of the six dimensions.

The six dimensions of price image covered in a comprehensive shopper-oriented pricing strategy include:

1. *Everyday shelf prices.* The strategy provides direction, including price-setting objectives and rules for the regular shelf prices shoppers see day in and day out.

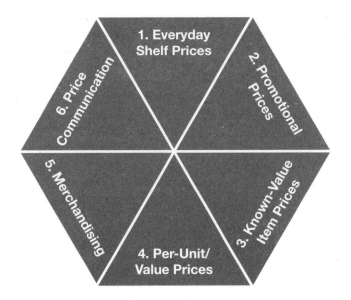

Figure 31.2 The six dimensions of price image

2. *Promotional prices.* The strategy must also determine the role that promotions play in the overall price mix at the total store level, eg high–low, everyday low price (EDLP) or a hybrid of high–low and EDLP, and how the promotions should be phased in at the department and category levels.
3. *Known-value item prices.* These represent the prices for the most important items in the store, ie the items for which shoppers are most likely to know the price, and that disproportionately affect price reputation. The strategy needs to identify the known-value items the retailer must price and manage carefully.
4. *Per-unit/value prices.* Price image is also influenced by the best values – measured on a price-per-unit-of-measure basis – available in each major category across the store. These best values are often provided by store brands. They appeal to 'specification buyers' who are willing to make brand trade-offs in a particular category to save money and stretch their grocery budgets. While few consumers shop this way in every category, most are willing to make trade-offs in search of strong per-unit values in some categories. A robust pricing strategy will determine the 'value', eg price per ounce, the retailer must offer in each category and how to get there.

Getting credit from shoppers for the low prices and strong values offered in dimensions 1 to 4 is critically important, yet often neglected by retailers. A successful pricing strategy must also provide direction in merchandising and price communication to capture 'shopper credit':

5. *Merchandising*. A comprehensive pricing strategy offers a plan for using the power of end-caps and other special displays to highlight great promotional prices and shelf merchandising to draw attention to strong values available in each category.
6. *Price communication*. Price communication is an essential yet largely overlooked driver of a retailer's price image. Many retailers spend thousands of staff hours and millions of dollars conducting sophisticated pricing analyses and implementing state-of-the-art pricing technology but are not positioned to receive full credit from shoppers for all their efforts and investment. Even retailers that have refined their price points to compete with the marketplace have to work diligently to get the word out to current and prospective shoppers.

Key elements of an effective price communication programme include:

- Holistic themes that clearly define the retailer's pricing efforts and clearly yet creatively show how consumers can be 'smart shoppers' and take advantage of all the great values available throughout the store.
- Shelf tags that draw attention to sale items or special prices and private label or value prices. This includes abundant 'compare against national brand' shelf tags that highlight the penny or dollar savings associated with purchasing a private label option. These tags are extremely effective at enhancing price image, even among shoppers who are not active in a particular category or who prefer branded items within the category. Just seeing all the different ways to save money – as highlighted in the shelf tags – strengthens price image and encourages consumers to shop in the store more intensively.
- Technology that facilitates targeted pricing, typically based on historical purchases captured through a loyalty marketing programme. Delivery vehicles for special, targeted offers include kiosks, touch-screen shopping carts, and even mobile phone programs that send text messages to shoppers with special offers during shopping trips.
- A disciplined, objective evaluative framework that allows retailers to assess their price communication efforts and compare them to those of key competitors.

Pricing has never been more important to retailers and shoppers than it is today. The best and brightest retailers around the world are determining their pricing tipping points and developing shopper-oriented, multidimensional pricing strategies designed to neutralize vulnerabilities, enhance price image and attract or retain shopper spending that drives profitable growth.

32 Packaging can be your best investment

Russ Napolitano

Russ Napolitano is executive vice president, business development, at Wallace Church, Inc. For over 30 years, Wallace Church has been renovating and innovating many leading global brands across all product categories through award-winning branding and package design.

When I mention such brands as Coca-Cola, Tide, Absolut, Method, Dove, Crayola and Simply Orange, to name just a few, there is a very good chance that an image of their packaging comes top of mind. When packages such as these become visual icons and such an important part of the brand's overall DNA, how can anyone argue that packaging cannot be one of your brand's smartest investments? Whether it is the physical package shape (its structure) or the colour, imagery or typography or a combination of these, many brands are identified by consumers through their packaging.

Packaging as your most efficient marketing investment

There is no doubt that we are facing some of the most challenging economic times in decades, and the events plaguing Wall Street and our pockets at the petrol pump are having an impact on consumer products goods companies, distributors, retailers and consumers. Costs to make, ship and distribute products have increased considerably recently. Companies are finding ways to do more without passing on the financial

Figure 32.1 Lean Cuisine

burden to their consumers. While packaging costs have also increased, you should realize that your brand's packaging is still one of your most efficient marketing tools for reaching your target consumers. You can still renovate or launch new packaging for less than 10 to 25 per cent of the total cost to produce a television advertisement, produce and run a print ad or execute a promotion and/or a display programme. Packaging will also have a longer shelf life, making it an even more cost-efficient method for reaching your consumers.

Packaging makes more of an impression

Not only will packaging have a longer shelf life than your advertising or promotions programme, but it will be seen by more people. Media spending is down for large and small brands, and media placements are more fragmented than ever. The average consumer is bombarded with anywhere from 250 to 5,000 media messages each day. It has become most challenging to connect with your consumer through any one medium, making it that much more difficult to reach your optimum level of media impressions. Consumers have more choices than ever – traditional media such as TV, magazines, newspapers and billboards, electronic media such as the internet, mobile phones, blogs and gaming, and 'word of mouth' (WOM). With stats like these, one might wonder how any brand could effectively and efficiently target its consumers these days.

Figure 32.2 Pop Stars

Through its package!

Is there any other vehicle that consumers interact with 24/7? From the time they notice your brand on the shelf and then purchase it, store it, use it and reuse it over and over again, they have formed a personal relationship with and an attachment to your brand through its package. Packaging is the one medium that results in a physical relationship with consumers.

The packaging also makes that first impression on the consumer. Consumers will often decide whether or not they are going to purchase your product through their first impression, which is usually made through the package.

Packaging is no longer strictly three-dimensional

Packaging creates a one-on-one personal experience that usually first takes place through sight. Imagine if your package incited some or most of the other four senses? Consumers have become very interested in packaging and, as a result, have high expectations. They want and expect packaging to entertain, engage and excite them on many levels. In developing your brand's packaging, understand if and how it can engage all of the five senses – sight, touch, sound, taste and smell. Delivering against the first is a must. Your package must have impact (sight) in order to break through the retail clutter and get noticed. Just imagine reinforcing sight with strong hand appeal (touch). Then you have managed to engage consumers on an even deeper level. Johnson's baby lotion took advantage of its 'baby soft skin' strategy by selecting the soft touch process for its bottles. When consumers pick up Johnson's baby lotion off the shelf, they are immediately reinforced with softness. There is nothing quite like having your product's end benefit engage consumers when they notice and pick up your package. Now, imagine if only the fragrance of Johnson's baby lotion can be infused in the bottle cap. It can. Just ask my friend Steven Landau at ScentSational Technologies.

Consumers have become more in tune with packaging

Consumers have become more in tune with packaging and have high expectations that their brand's packaging is going to meet both their functional and their emotional needs. Of course the package must be easy to carry, hold and store. But it must also be easy to use, reuse and discard. Major companies are starting to take packaging more seriously because of the demands imposed on them by their consumers. Procter & Gamble, Johnson & Johnson, GlaxoSmithKline, HJ Heinz, Pepsi and Nestlé are just a small fraction of the companies that have internal design teams solely responsible for making sure that both structural and graphic design are given the attention they need and deserve within each brand's marketing mix. P&G successfully disproved conventional wisdom when it redesigned its Olay packaging to be more reminiscent of packaging that is usually found in higher-end department stores. Up to this point, there had been an 'unwritten theory' that consumers would never spend more than $18 for any skincare item distributed in mass outlets. This price point was reserved for department or prestige outlets. When P&G redesigned the structural and graphic packaging for Olay, its goal was to position the brand as prestige skin care that was now available via the convenience of your neighbourhood drugstore. P&G took a bold step in laying the groundwork for new opportunities and setting the stage for higher expectations at mass retail. There is no doubt that this premium price point is contributing to Olay's overall return on investment.

We cannot ignore that another major reason that consumers are more connected to packaging is the fact that they are also more in tune with what is happening in the world around them. Consumers know that packaging is one of the biggest culprits when it comes to increased consumer waste. Consumer products good companies, manufacturers and consumers must all work together to identify alternative resources and materials responsibly. Less is more. Several studies have shown that consumers would be willing to pay more for one product that is deemed 'environmentally friendly' versus one that is not.

You must stay in tune with your packaging

Just as consumers have become more conscious of packaging, you must also stay in tune with your brand's packaging. It used to be true that a newly designed package would last five to eight years. Most packages today are updated or 'freshened' every two to three years. Why? The competition! If you are paying more attention to packaging, so are your competitors. If you want to maintain a leadership position, you have to make sure that your packaging positions your brand as the leader and stays relevant to consumers. Consumers are fickle and their needs and habits are changing frequently. If you ignore this fact, others will pass you by. You must keep one eye looking forward and one looking back, because you never know who is about to pass you by or who is right on your tail.

Figure 32.3 Ivory Pure

In addition to worrying about your existing competitive pool, there is always someone new waiting in the wings about to make a big and lasting impression. Don't believe me? Just ask P&G. Did P&G ever think that someone like Method would come along and turn the dish care category upside down? Method took dish care out from under the sink and proudly displayed it on the counter. Those of us who thought that Method would stay in the kitchen were fooled yet again. Method is now a household name (and in a relatively short period of time by conventional standards), with products represented in every household category from hand washing to floor cleaning and from laundry to air care. Watch out Johnson's Baby. Method Baby has arrived at a store near you.

How did Method accomplish such success and become a household name? Simply through great design. Method's mantra is to infiltrate every room in the house through product design that becomes part of your home's decor. Method has successfully taken what has been viewed as very functional categories and made them emotional, engaging many of our senses. They have taken the household 'chores' and made them more motivating. Oh, and by the way, did I tell you that Method has achieved this without any advertising?

For many products, packaging is their sole form of advertising

Let's face it. In prosperous times and in economically challenging times, packaging is the sole form of advertising for many brands. Some brands can and never will be able to afford to advertise, others will have their advertising budgets reduced and still others don't believe advertising is necessary. Why? They believe that the package is their best form of advertising. They view packaging as the most valuable form of real estate. Seize this opportunity. Take the time and money

Figure 32.4 Ciao Bella

to do it right. It frustrates me no end when marketers will allocate the least amount of money toward the one thing that makes the biggest impression on consumers – the package. Again, I dare you to find a smarter investment.

Packaging as the 'fifth P' in your marketing mix

Marketing 101 teaches us all about the importance of the 'four Ps' when marketing a product – product, price, place and promotion. We are taught how these 'four Ps' are critical whether we are launching, maintaining or restaging a product. What about the role of the package in the marketing mix? Anyone who is marketing a product whose contents require a container must factor in the role that packaging plays. One could argue that packaging is one of the most critical factors contributing to a brand's success, so much so that it should become the 'fifth P'. After all, the life cycle of the package is longer than that of some of the other Ps. A typical package life cycle consists of development, filling, shipping, storage, shelf placement, shopping cart, home transportation, storage, usage and finally some kind of discarding (hopefully recycling). Any one thing with such an extensive life cycle should be given the highest of priorities.

Increased role of shopper marketing

The new buzz in town is all about shopper marketing and the role the retail environment plays in capturing the consumer's attention. This encompasses merchandising practices, displays, in-store communications and promotions. There is lots of talk around the impact of shopper marketing on influencing consumers' purchasing habits. Extensive studies have shown the effectiveness of shopper marketing. Would anyone care to venture a guess as to which vehicle is considered to be among those having the most impact? Yes, the package. Packaging plays an integral role and has a major impact on shopper marketing. When a consumer is walking down an aisle and stumbles upon a shelf talker, floor ad or end-aisle display, it is the packaging that will often result in that first moment of truth – the purchase decision. For many brands the packaging usually sets the tone for all of the other communications efforts, establishing the brand's overall look and feel. Sounds like a pretty smart choice to me.

33 Six principles to drive effective packaging

Scott Young

Scott Young is the president of Perception Research Services International, a company that conducts over 600 studies annually to help develop, assess and improve packaging systems – and to help marketers 'win at retail'.

Designing for the shopper: six principles to drive effective packaging

We are often asked for 'dos and don'ts' of effective packaging, based on our experience across thousands of consumer research studies. Although this may appear to be a simple question, it is actually quite difficult to generalize about 'what works' across product categories, countries and retail channels. In fact, we often find that 'breaking the rules' (through revolutionary designs that diverge from a category's visual norms) is exactly what creates differentiation and drives success. For example, Wrigley's new '5' gum has been successful through black (and somewhat cryptic or mysterious) packaging that contrasts greatly with the traditional, colourful packaging of the category.

While it is not possible to reduce package design to a formula, our experience suggests that there are several core principles that are consistently linked to successful design, regardless of whether we are studying hair care sachets in Indian kiosks or cereals in European hypermarkets. In this chapter, I'll discuss these principles – and offer several positive examples of their application.

Design for visibility

First and foremost, package design should start with the realization that clutter is the universal reality of the shopping experience. Therefore, the first challenge for any packaging system is to consistently 'break through clutter' to generate shoppers' consideration. In fact, our PRS Eye-Tracking studies suggest that shoppers never even see two-thirds of the products on the shelf, even when they are actively shopping in a category.

On a broader level, designing for visibility involves understanding the merchandising environment in which packaging appears, recognizing you often have limited control of how packages are actually presented – and designing for the worst-case scenario. Perhaps the most common example is the fact that packages are often not stocked properly. In other words, we can't assume that front panels will be facing forward, so packaging needs to communicate branding on all panels.

Shelf visibility – what works?

When it comes to visibility, the one-word answer is contrast. It's not a question of what people want to look at, but rather a matter of physiology – and items that differentiate draw the eye. Certainly, colour blocking (such as the green wall of Fructis) is a very powerful strategy for creating visual contrast and brand recognition. Specifically, we've found that colour blocking (ie 'owning a colour') is particularly important for new products or smaller brands with limited facings.

In addition to colour, we've seen several other effective strategies for visibility, including the use of a strong brand mark or visual icon and the effective use of negative or white space, all of which are evident on Special K packaging. As this example illustrates, in a world

Figure 33.1 Example, design for shop-ability: hair care shelf

Figure 33.2 Example, design for visibility: chewing gum shelf

of 'screaming' packages, it is simplicity that creates contrast and draws attention and involvement.

Design for shop-ability

A second (and related) reality of the shopping experience is that people are overwhelmed by too many choices at retail. We've seen that, in addition to creating confusion and frustration, this overabundance of choice leads many shoppers to 'default to the familiar' (ie buy their old brand, rather than taking the time to consider new choices). This phenomenon – and the aforementioned challenge of retail visibility – helps to explain why new product failure rates are so high.

Designing for shop-ability goes beyond simply helping shoppers find 'their product' quickly and accurately (ie findability). It's also important to ensure that shoppers can quickly and clearly understand relationships among products (ie product differentiation). While findability is certainly important to those shoppers who know what they want, effective product differentiation – conveying the unique feature or benefit of each product within a line – is actually what drives shoppers to 'trade up' to higher-end products and/or make incremental purchases.

Shop-ability – what works?

To facilitate shop-ability, designers should think primarily in terms of continuity, rather than differentiation. Specifically, it's important to have a consistent layout of information delivery across packages, so that shoppers can easily pick up and compare two packages (in terms of key features, benefits, usage occasions, etc). Conversely, when packages have different layouts, it is more difficult for shoppers to make these comparisons. Similarly, a 'build effect' (eg adding an extra bullet) can be very effective in conveying different quality levels across products. When one package has three claims and another has three very different claims, it can be challenging to understand their relationship.

Of course, people do tend to shop by colour (eg 'I buy the Tropicana with the blue cap'), so the effective and intuitive use of colour-coding is also important, particularly in terms of conveying flavour or scent or implying quality level (gold, silver, etc). However, we have consistently seen that partial colour-coding (via caps, flags, etc) can be just as effective as having packages fully colour-coded (eg a yellow pack, a green pack, etc). Thus, it is possible both to 'own a colour' (for retail visibility) and to use colour-coding effectively (to facilitate shopping).

Finally, across studies, we've found that the use of sub-brands (particularly more abstract options such as 'plus', 'total', 'extra', etc) often hinders shop-ability, by adding an additional layer of copy that doesn't add useful information. Therefore it's important to ensure that sub-brands and product names speak to features or benefits.

Figure 33.3 Example, design for shop-ability: tropicana shelf

Figure 33.4 Example, design for differentiation: Discreet

Design for differentiation (on a visceral level)

It's also important to remember that packaging communication is primarily visual and that purchase decisions are often intuitive and emotional rather than fact based. In addition, packaging is inherently comparative in nature, as competitors are typically nearby on the shelf. These factors make it critical for packaging to 'own' or 'embody' a key dimension on an immediate and intuitive level, without relying on copy or claims. In other words, your packaging needs to look more effective, more refreshing, more healthy, more authentic or perhaps more high-tech than the competition at first glance. In addition, if the packaging does not look and feel appetizing, claims will not convince people otherwise.

Differentiation – what works?

Across regions, we've often found that packaging structure (particularly unique shapes and delivery systems) can be a very powerful weapon for differentiation. In fact, while package colour and logo often link to brand visibility and recognition, a unique shape can send a strong implied brand or product message. For example, 3M's recent introduction of plastic packaging for Nexcare bandages sent a strong message of innovation and category leadership (relative to Band-Aid), which drove double-digit sales gains.

Of course, packaging graphics can also be used to drive differentiation if they represent a significant break from category norms, as in Pepsi's recent adoption of rotating packaging graphics. However, it's also important to keep the category's ultimate purpose or end-benefit in mind: if you are designing for efficacy-driven categories (cat litter, dishwashing detergent, etc), the packaging still has to look effective!

Figure 33.5 Example, design for a single clear message: Nexcare

Design for a single clear message

When shoppers do pick up a package, they typically spend very little time deciding if it should head into the shopping cart. For this reason, we've nearly always found that 'less is more' in terms of packaging copy – and that it is best to highlight a single clear message or claim. In fact, PRS Eye-Tracking studies show that, typically, in the approximately five seconds spent examining a package, shoppers take in only three to four design elements (the branding, the main visual, a product descriptor and perhaps one claim). In addition, we've seen that adding copy (such as an extra claim) does not consistently lead to longer viewing time. Therefore, if a package is cluttered with many claims or design elements, they will simply fight for attention – and no single message will consistently come across.

Messaging – what works?

For package messaging, the one-word answer is simplicity. Typically, the key to simplicity lies in identifying a single strong 'point-of-difference' message – and ensuring that secondary claims and/or product information fall outside the primary package viewing flow. It's also important to combine design elements when possible, by ensuring that necessary elements (such as the brand logo or product name) also convey key features and benefits. The effective use of visual icons can also promote simplicity, by reducing copy, particularly on multilingual packages.

However, it is important to avoid crossing over the line from simple to stark or sterile: we've frequently found that very sparse white packaging can be polarizing, as it can be perceived as generic. This is one area in which the prevailing design aesthetic varies widely by region, as Europeans tend to associate simplicity with sophistication, while Asians favour busier packaging.

Figure 33.6 Russian viewing pattern

Design to drive consumption

Once packaging makes it home, its shape and structure play a significant (and obvious) role in driving functionality (ease of holding, dispensing, etc), satisfaction and repurchase. What's less obvious and equally important, however, is the impact of packaging in driving consumption rates. Specifically, we've seen that where a product is stored in the home (in the refrigerator versus in the pantry, or on the table versus in the closet, etc) has a direct impact on how frequently it is consumed. In the store, unseen is unsold. In the home, unseen is unused.

Driving consumption – what works?

Many recent 'success stories' (of packaging driving sales), such as fridge packs, have been tied to helping packaging 'live' within the refrigerator. Similarly, packaging that creates constant product visibility (on the counter, in the bathroom, etc) can serve as a brand reminder in the home.

A second effective strategy for driving consumption lies in packaging that allows for brands to extend to new usage situations. Perhaps the most prevalent example is 'on-the-go' packaging (for snacks, confectionery, etc), which is designed for consumption in cars. However, we've also seen new packaging forms (such as Go-Gurts and 100 Calorie Packs) that have extended categories into new usage occasions (school lunches, etc).

Figure 33.7 Example, design to drive consumption: Heinz

Figure 33.8 Example, design to drive consumption: Coke fridge pack

Design for sustainability

Finally, designers should recognize increasing shopper sensitivity to environmental concerns. While most sustainable packaging initiatives have been developed in response to retailer requirements (such as the Wal-Mart environmental scorecard), there's no doubt that shoppers are becoming more environmentally aware – and are potentially willing to reward companies that take the lead in introducing more environmentally friendly packaging. However, our studies suggest that there is a significant 'knowledge gap' that gets in the way: most shoppers simply don't know which packaging systems and materials are better for the environment. Therefore, in addition to developing more environmentally friendly solutions, marketers and designers need to work on conveying these benefits clearly on packs, by using terminology that shoppers understand.

Sustainability – what works?

Across categories, we've repeatedly seen that packaging sustainability and functionality are not mutually exclusive. In fact, reducing packaging materials (through the elimination of secondary packaging, for example) can often help marketers deliver key end-benefits (such as the ability to see the product).

In terms of messaging, we've found that most shoppers define their environmental responsibility in terms of recycling – and that a small icon (on the bottom of a package) is often not enough to provide this reassurance. Most importantly, the environmental message has to be conveyed clearly, in language that shoppers can understand. Specifically, we've found that terms such as 'post-consumer materials' and even 'sustainability' create confusion. In addition, we've found that environmental packaging claims best resonate when linked to 'green' product propositions, such as Clorox's Green Works line of cleaning products.

Figure 33.9 Example, design for sustainability: Clorox Green Works

Driving success: including the shopper in the design process

Many of the 'shopper design' principles I've outlined above are quite intuitive – and I suspect that few would be actively challenged or debated. However, the reality is that very few companies actively incorporate these principles in their process to make packaging decisions.

Despite the importance of shelf visibility and shop-ability, many packaging systems are developed and assessed apart from the shelf context (via consumer feedback from focus groups and web-based studies). And, despite the importance of conveying a clear singular message, many packaging systems are cluttered with multiple claims (because marketers are reluctant to prioritize).

Therefore, as we look to advise clients on developing effective packaging, the core answer is that what works consistently is a packaging development and assessment process that centres on the shopper. This best-practice process will integrate these key principles by:

- including the shelf context in packaging development and research, when showing design systems both to shoppers and to marketing managers;
- integrating shopper understanding in the packaging development process, to identify which packaging messages or claims it is most important to prioritize;
- approaching packaging sustainability efforts in a holistic manner, which addresses shoppers' functional priorities and information needs.

Across brands, markets and design initiatives, companies that build these shopper design principles into their way of doing business are likely to be well rewarded at the shelf.

34 How to maximize ROI with package promotions

Ville Maila

Ville Maila is the planning director for Phenomena Group, in charge of planning package promotions and developing new promotion mechanisms. Phenomena Group was the first shopper marketing company founded in Europe. Phenomena specializes in shopper marketing campaigns and is the global leader in packaging promotions operating in over 40 countries.

Is the package of daily consumer goods a mass medium?

In communication, media (singular Medium) are the storage and transmission tools used to store and deliver information or data. It is often referred to as synonymous with mass media.
http://en.wikipedia.org/wiki/Media_(communication)

Mass media is a term used to denote a section of the media specifically envisioned and designed to reach a very large audience such as the population of a nation state.
http://en.wikipedia.org/wiki/Mass_media

What is the most cost-efficient form of in-store campaigning?

During their visit to a store, shoppers are faced with tens (if not hundreds) of thousands of messages trying to persuade them to buy, but on average only 10–20 of these messages will lead to a purchase decision. Almost everyone visits stores weekly and therefore your most important medium, the communication on the packages, will reach a majority. In the store, the package promotion is a means to stand out among competing in-store media communication. The package promotion is a campaign that does not require any special measures from the personnel, and it is a cost-efficient way to achieve up to 100 per cent selling distribution. Note that packaging is the only medium of communication in the store that still can be controlled by the supplier. Retailers are nowadays in charge of other in-store communication and campaigns.

Phase one: choose the most profitable objective

Do you aim at purchase frequency or penetration?

When choosing the objective of package promotion, you must first calculate which objective is more profitable – purchase frequency or penetration. The chosen objective dictates how the promotion mechanism affects shoppers' buying behaviour. Objective-specification is the most important factor influencing the profitability of package promotion, since the promotion mechanism cannot have an effective impact on increasing penetration and purchase frequency at the same time.

Calculate the profit prognosis before choosing the objective

The objective is chosen by calculating the profit prognosis regarding increasing both penetration and purchase frequency, based on the product's present annual sales, penetration and purchase frequency. As regards annual sales, radical changes in the product assortment that have occurred during the measuring period must also be accounted for. With the help of the formulae in Figures 34.1 to 34.4, you can evaluate which of the objectives is most profitable for the current market situation of your brand.

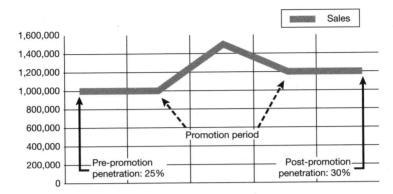

Figure 34.1 Impact of penetration promotion on sales

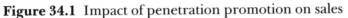

Figure 34.2 Penetration

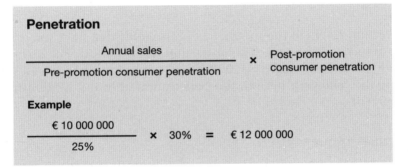

Figure 34.3 Impact of purchase frequency promotion on sales

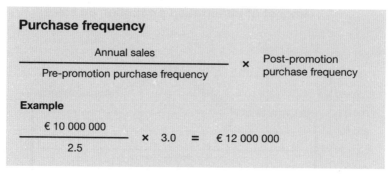

Figure 34.4 Purchase frequency

Concepts from ACNielsen Insight: using panels to understand the consumer

Penetration

Penetration refers to the number of households that have purchased the product at least once during the follow-up period. For example, if 5,000 households out of 10,000 have bought brand X at least once during the follow-up period, the penetration of brand X amounts to 50 per cent.

Purchase frequency

Purchase frequency is defined by calculating the average number of purchases made by consumers during the follow-up period. For instance, if 5,000 households out of 10,000 have bought brand X 10,000 times, the purchase frequency of brand X is 2.0.

Phase two: choose the most effective promotion mechanism

The chosen objective determines the promotion mechanism

Defining the objective determines the promotion mechanisms that drive the chosen goals. The promotion mechanism cannot have an effective impact on both penetration and increased purchase frequency at the same time. For example, a collection premium effectively enhances purchasing frequency, but is ineffective in increasing penetration, whereas a satisfaction guarantee increases penetration but not purchasing frequency. Among the promotion mechanisms that drive the defined objective, it's most advantageous to select the most cost-effective option.

Phenomena's competence is based on statistics

Phenomena has analysed almost all the package promotions it has planned during the period June 2003 to January 2008. The results of the survey are found from the matrices in Figures 34.5 and 34.6. The matrices depict the sales impacts of different package promotion mechanisms on the increase in purchasing frequencies and penetration in relation to the costs of the promotion. The research data consisted of the cost structure of more than 150 promotions, as well as their impact on the increase in the promoted product's purchasing frequency and penetration.

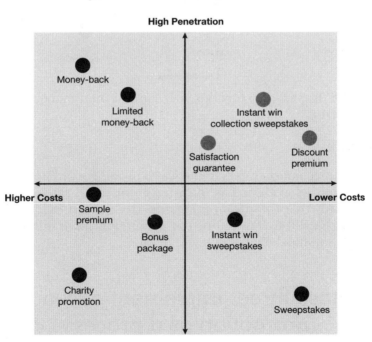

Figure 34.5 Impact of promotion mechanisms on penetration in relation to costs

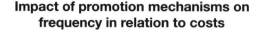

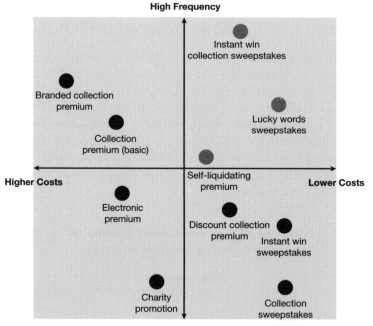

Figure 34.6 Impact of promotion mechanisms on frequency in relation to costs

Concepts

Promotion mechanism refers to the way a promotion influences shoppers' buying behaviour. The starting point in all sales-increasing promotions is that the promotion generates at least one additional purchasing decision. Therefore the promotion mechanism defines how the promotion behaves in terms of sales.

Phase three: implement package promotion as a process

Brief

The most important element of a successful brief is a single clearly specified objective. The objective can be one of the two options:

increasing penetration or increasing purchasing frequency. The objective should be chosen by calculating the profit prognosis for both increased penetration and increased purchasing frequency, based on the product's current annual sales, penetration and purchasing frequency. Descriptions of the brand and the target group are required for background information. Additionally, the brief should include a general description of the category's development and the shoppers' buying behaviour and an analysis of the past promotions' efficiency.

Mechanism analysis

Mechanism analysis helps to clarify which promotion mechanism contributes to achieving the defined objectives most efficiently. After this, a legal due diligence is made, which helps to clarify how the chosen promotion mechanism can be implemented in the chosen market areas. In addition, the cost-effectiveness of the chosen mechanism is optimized: for example, the number of collection premiums and promotion packages needed; how many collection tokens consumers should collect; the value of the premiums; and the desired redemption value of the premiums required to obtain the defined objectives.

Promotion design

The key basis for shopper-driven promotion design is planning the kind of promotional message and visual outlook that support the brand, stop the consumer and induce shoppers' purchasing decisions. The first step in the design process is to specify all the elements of the promotion. This step is followed by setting clear objectives for the various components. The elements to be specified consist of: added value to shoppers (such as a prize or a premium); the promotion mechanism; in-store materials; supporting media; and sales support materials for sales to the trade.

Implementing promotion elements

In the implementation stage of the promotion elements, the key issue is to design a visual outlook that supports the brand and stops the shopper at the point of sale. Individual components are produced ready for the launch, promotional materials for different markets are localized, the required acquisition of materials is made, and the final promotion elements are delivered to the distribution and sales channels of the different market areas.

Final analysis

After the promotion, the resulting statistics are collated into a PowerPoint presentation. The analysis presents numerically how well the different elements of the promotion obtained the market-area- and distribution-channel-specific objectives.

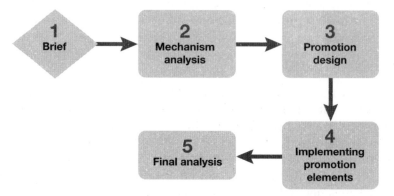

Figure 34.7 Implementing package promotion as a process

Index

NB: page numbers in *italic* indicate figures or tables